Samuel Pasfield Oliver

Off Duty. Rambles of a Gunner

Through Nicaragua, January to June, 1867

Samuel Pasfield Oliver

Off Duty. Rambles of a Gunner
Through Nicaragua, January to June, 1867

ISBN/EAN: 9783744746175

Printed in Europe, USA, Canada, Australia, Japan

Cover: Foto ©ninafisch / pixelio.de

More available books at **www.hansebooks.com**

OFF DUTY.

RAMBLES OF A GUNNER.

THROUGH NICARAGUA,

JANUARY TO JUNE, 1867.

S. P. O.

LONDON:
PRINTED BY TAYLOR AND FRANCIS, RED LION COURT, FLEET STREET.
1879.

OFF DUTY.

RAMBLES OF A GUNNER.

THROUGH NICARAGUA,
JANUARY TO JUNE, 1867.

S. P. O.

LONDON:
PRINTED BY TAYLOR AND FRANCIS, RED LION COURT, FLEET STREET.
1879.

ALERE FLAMMAM.

PRINTED BY TAYLOR AND FRANCIS,
RED LION COURT, FLEET STREET.

INTRODUCTORY.

Since attention has lately been called to an international transit-route across the isthmus which joins the two Americas, I have found still by me my Diary of a journey across that tract of country which is deemed the best route for a canal by the most competent of modern American engineers. In order, therefore, to give some idea of the country to be traversed, I have put in type the following chapter, relating one of a gunner's numerous rambles, on and off duty, in both hemispheres.

The (so-called) International Congress of 1879, for deciding on the question of an interoceanic canal across the American isthmus was opened in Paris, under the ostensible auspices of the Geographical Society of Paris; I say "ostensible" advisedly, as it was clear from the commencement that the meeting was organized by M. Lesseps, who was nominated president by Admiral de la Roncière.

The following is a brief account of the International Congress :—

Paris, May 15.

The International Congress for the discussion of the various schemes which have been projected for cutting a canal through the Isthmus of Panama, met to-day in Paris. Admiral de la Roncière-le-Noury opened the proceedings by a speech explaining the object which the Congress had in view, and thanking the foreign Powers for having replied to the appeal of France by sending representatives to Paris to take part in the deliberations of the Congress. He also referred in terms of high praise to the energy and skill of M. de Lesseps, and concluded by pointing to the peaceful aims of the Congress.

M. de Lesseps was then requested to assume the presidency of the Congress, and Sir John Stokes, the English representative, Admiral Ammon, the United States delegate, Signor Christoforo Negri, the Italian delegate, and Admiral Likhatscheff, the Russian commissioner, were nominated Vice-Presidents.

All the Powers to which the appeal of the French Government on the subject was addressed have sent representatives, and the name of each delegate, as it was called by the secretary, was received with loud applause.

The secretary subsequently read a paper treating at length the whole question before the meeting, and the Congress, after resolving to divide itself into five committees to discuss the various branches of the proposed undertaking, finally adjourned until Monday next.

Paris, May 19.

The second sitting of the Congress convened for the purpose of discussing the practicability of constructing a canal uniting the Atlantic and Pacific Oceans took place to-day. A letter was read from Captain Bedford Pim, M.P., regretting his inability to be present. M. de Lesseps, the President, stated that the labours of the Congress were progressing rapidly, and would probably be concluded by Sunday or Monday next.

A grand international banquet was subsequently held at the Continental Hotel, at the conclusion of which M. Fontanes read a report, which, after giving the history of the Suez Canal, pointed out that, in order to make sure of the success of the Interoceanic Canal, it would be necessary that 6,000,000 tons of shipping should pass through it yearly, or a daily passage of eight ships of 2050 tons each. It was calculated that after the harvest sixteen vessels would pass through the Canal daily. The report also stated that the Canal would be capable of allowing the passage of fifty vessels at a time. It condemned the idea of erecting locks, a single one of which would reduce to twenty-four the number of vessels capable of passing through the Canal. A system of locks would, therefore, compromise the success of the undertaking. M. Simonin presented another report, pointing out the advantages which the commerce of all nations would derive from the canal, and the increase which would result in the trade of producers of grain. He stated that the fifth committee lacked the documents necessary for suggesting a tariff and estimating the general revenue, but would send in its report to-morrow.

The Technical Commission of the Interoceanic Congress met to-day to hear reports from its two sub-committees, the second of which admitted the possibility of constructing a canal with locks by way of Nicaragua, while, for a level canal, it considered the course proposed by Lieutenants Wyse and Reclus to be the best, subject, however, to certain modifications.

The first sub-committee presented estimates of the probable cost of the various routes.

The Tehuantepec line would, it was calculated, require an outlay of a milliard of francs, without reckoning for the construction of ports; the cost of carrying out the Nicaragua project of Ménocal was estimated at 7,111,000,000f.; the plan of Lieutenants Wyse and Reclus at 1,065,000,000f., plus the indemnity to the railway; and the Atrato-Napipi scheme at 1,100,000,000f. The committee stated that it was impossible to give any precise estimate for the Blanchet proposal.

The Statistical Commission on the projected Interoceanic Canal has published its report, which estimates the goods actually in transit at 4,830,000 tons, adding, however, that an increase of 6 per cent. in the navigation would, within ten years of the opening of the canal, raise the tonnage to 7,250,000.

The Fifth Commission demands payment of a transit duty of 15f. per ton, which would be reduced in proportion to the increase in the traffic. The gross receipts of the canal are estimated at 90,000,000f., and, after pay-

ing the total interest due to the creditors, it is believed a sum of 42,000,000f. would remain for the redemption of the Company's bonds and other unforeseen expenses. The Commission is opposed to receiving assistance from any Government, and requires the Interoceanic Congress to declare the canal absolutely neutral, except in case of war.

The Commercial Commission has not yet taken any decision on the subject, considering the proposed transit duty of 15f. too high, especially for sailing vessels.

At the sitting of the Interoceanic Canal Congress to-day, Sir John Hawkshaw called attention to the danger of inundations of the river Chagres if the Panama scheme were adopted. This river runs almost parallel to the present Aspinwall and Panama railway. Sir John Hawkshaw believes that in the wet season the current is five miles an hour, and that were the canal carried through a tunnel, the latter might be entirely filled with water. M. Reclus combated this view, and another member argued that the Atrato-Nipipi route was free from any such danger.

Paris, May 29.

The Panama Canal Congress terminated its sittings to-day, when Voisin Bey read the report of the Technical Committee on the seven schemes which it had considered. The nature, probable cost, &c. of them it thus summarized: —The Tehuantepec, 240 kilomètres, 120 sluices, 12 days transit. Nicaragua, Ménocal-Blanchet schemes, each 292 kilomètres, 17 sluices; cost of construction, including sluices, 770,000,000f.; total cost 900,000,000f.; 4½ days. Panama, level canal, 73 kilomètres, 1 sluice, 6 kilomètres of tunnel; construction 1,070,000,000f.; total coast 1,200,000,000f.; 2 days. Panama, sluices, 73 kilomètres, 12 sluices; construction 570,000,000f.; total cost 700,000,000f.; 2 days. San Blas, 53 kilomètres, 16 kilomètres of tunnel; construction 1,270,000,000f.; total cost 1,400,000,000; 1 day. Atrato Napipi, 290 kilomètres, 2 sluices, 4 kilomètres of tunnel; construction 1,000,000,000f.; total cost 1,130,000,000f; 3 days. The expense of working and repairs was set down in each case, capitalized at 5 per cent., at 130,000,000f. As to the Tehuantepec route, the committee had no data on which to estimate the cost, but believed it would greatly exceed that of any of the other schemes. The Nicaragua project offered an inexhaustible reservoir of water, and a port could easily be made on the Pacific side; but serious difficulties were to be apprehended at certain points. The Panama schemes offered excellent ports at both ends, and the existing railway would facilitate the transit of material. Subject to tidal sluice at the Pacific end, and the complete isolation of the waters of the Charges and its affluents, the level scheme was quite satisfactory. The Darien projects were not acceptable. The Committee objected also to the Nicaragua scheme, though technically feasible, on account of the volcanic nature of the country and consequent liability to destruction of the work. The Panama route, on the other hand, had long been free from volcanic action, and was decidedly preferable above

all others. The choice lay here between a level canal and one with sluices, and the Committee decidedly preferred the former. A report was likewise presented by the President and office-bearers of the Congress at large and those of the various committees. This document cited the Suez Canal traffic and charges as proof of the remunerativeness of the enterprise, and advocated a flat canal, through which fifty ships could pass daily, and capable of sheltering at least sixty ships at a time. It recommended the Congress to adopt the following resolution:—

"The Congress holds that the cutting of an interoceanic canal of uniform level (a work so desirable in the interest of commerce and navigation) is practicable, and that the maritime canal, in order to meet the indispensable facilities of access and utilization which ought to be offered by a passage of this kind, should be made from the Gulf of Limon to the Bay of Panama."

The roll was then called, and each member of the Congress was asked to vote upon the resolution. M. de Lesseps was warmly cheered on voting in its favour, and Sir John Stokes also voted affirmatively. The resolution was carried by 74 to 8, there being 16 abstentions*. M. de Lesseps, on relinquishing the chair to Admiral la Roncière-le-Noury, expressed the pleasure with which he had taken part in this first engagement, and his readiness to put forward any further efforts in behalf of the enterprise. Admiral la Roncière-le-Noury then dismissed the Congress with a brief speech, in which he dwelt on the interest taken in the canal by the Paris Geographical Society, under whose auspices the Congress had met, and hoped M. de Lesseps might live to see this second isthmus as successfully cut through as that of Suez had been. To-night the members of the Congress have been received by President Grévy at the Elysée.

But meantime the United States delegates had returned to America, not disappointed at the rejection of their Nicaraguan route, as they well knew what was forthcoming and had not voted; but on their arrival made their report to Mr. Evarts, Secretary of State, for the information of the United States House of Representatives, and transmitted to the House by the President on the 13th of June, which report gives a history of the negotiations with the Central American States relative to intercommunication between the two oceans, and concludes as follows:—

"The latest step taken by this Government has been the sending of two Commissioners to take part in the Interoceanic Canal Congress, which met at Paris on the 15th ult., under the auspices of the Geographical Society of

---

* Of the English and American members of the Congress, Sir John Stokes and Messrs. Appleton, Lazard, and Christiansen voted for the scheme; Sir Charles Hartley, Admiral Ammon, and Messrs. Bell, Lobnitz, Johnston, Smith, and Ménocal abstained from voting; and Sir John Hawkshaw and Messrs. Lewis, Evans, and Selfridge were absent. This foredetermined resolution of the Congress was, as had been predicted, the precursor of a French speculation, which was soon announced in the papers as follows:—"M. de Lesseps, it is understood, will shortly issue a prospectus inviting subscriptions for the Panama Canal, and will repair thither in September."

that city, and under the immediate direction of M. Ferdinand de Lesseps, the successful engineer of the Suez Canal. Pursuant to the unofficial invitation tendered by M. de Lesseps, the President designated Rear-Admiral Daniel Ammon and Civil Engineer Aniceto G. Ménocal, both of the navy, to take part in the deliberations of that Congress; but they were not authorized to commit this Government to any engagement, either as to the choice of the route or the assumption of any material guarantee for the expense of constructing the canal. It is understood that the high character of these officers and the knowledge of the subject acquired by them in repeated surveys and explorations over the different routes caused their views to be received with attention. Their report of the proceedings and conclusions of the Congress has not yet been received. The policy of the United States on the general subject of isthmian transit is understood to have been, and to be, not to undertake the construction of a ship-canal on its own account, even if the practicability of such a work, at a reasonable cost, were to be shown, but to secure by treaties protection to the capital of such citizens as may be disposed to embark in the enterprise. It will be my purpose to give an attentive consideration to whatever may pass in other commercial countries relative to this subject, and to omit no favourable opportunity for useful negotiations in behalf of the interests of this Government and the commercial enterprise of its citizens."

The American newspapers criticized somewhat unfavourably the proceedings of the recent Darien Canal Congress at Paris, indicating that but little assistance for the enterprise, under its present auspices, could be expected from Americans.

Admiral Ammon, United States' Commissioner to the Canal Congress, reports to the Secretary of State on the various foreign projects presented for a canal, and makes severe strictures upon the schemes of foreign engineers, and the manner in which they ignored the practical surveys by American engineers. *Admiral Ammon characterizes the action of the foreign Commissioners as a well-laid scheme by them to control this highway,* adding that, unless the United States acts promptly, this great commercial enterprise will be controlled by the European Powers, and American trade be at the mercy of any discriminating regulations those Governments may impose.

Senator Burnside introduced a resolution in the Senate reaffirming the Monroe doctrine :—"That the nations of the American Continent are not to be considered subjects for future domination by any European Power ; and declaring that the people of the United States would not view without serious inquietude any attempt by the European Powers to establish under their protection or domination a ship-canal across the Isthmus of Darien, and that such action could not be regarded in any other light than as a manifestation of unfriendly disposition towards the United States." The resolution was referred to the Foreign Committee.

Meantime the following paragraphs, all so many advertisements, appeared in the public papers :—

"M. de Lesseps starts for London on Wednesday, and will probably be present at the banquet given by the Lord Mayor to the Society for the Protection of Copyright. It is likely that M. de Lesseps will take advantage of this and any other opportunity to explain his project for cutting through the Isthmus of Panama. He is already known to be resolved on launching this colossal enterprise, involving a capital of £16,000,000 sterling, and to have declared he will be present on the 1st of January next at the beginning of the work. The English public will soon know, through M. de Lesseps himself, to what point he counts on the success of his new undertaking."

We next find M. de Lesseps at the Guildhall and at other public banquets advocating his schemes:—

"M. de Lesseps, replying in French, said that when he came to England in 1870 he had the honour of being made a citizen of London, and he was then told that if England had not found the capital for the construction of the Suez Canal, she would pay the interest in the tolls that would be received from her ships passing through the canal. Remembering the success which had attended that undertaking, he thought that the English people should now feel some confidence in the enterprise in which he was about to engage. But the people of this country should not only show their interest in the project by sending their ships through the canal when it had been constructed, they should at once take shares. The English had been the great supporters of the Suez Canal. They were courageous—he might say audacious —in their maritime enterprises; they had entirely changed the system of navigation by adopting steam instead of sailing vessels, and they were really paying the interest of the shares of the Suez Canal by contributing 100,000 francs per day in tolls. He was sure that the cutting of the Panama Canal would be finished in eight years, and in September he should invite all the world to subscribe to the enterprise. To that call he had no doubt he should receive a general and ready response. He drank success to the cutting of the canal, and prosperity to the great English nation."

Lyons, July 10.

The Press of this city gave a breakfast yesterday to M. Ferdinand de Lesseps, who, in acknowledging the toast of his health, expressed confidence in the success of the Panama Canal project, and the future of other great schemes for facilitating international communication, such as the proposed Central Asian railway and the fertilization of the Sahara region.

Mr. Nathan Appleton, an American, replying to the toast of the United States, said the country of George Washington would give unlimited assistance to the country of Lafayette, and declared, in conclusion, that America would heartily second the French undertaking for the construction of the Panama Canal.

M. de Lesseps, at a dinner given to him last night, M. Isaac Pereira being one of the speakers, stated that the Panama Canal scheme, to be launched this month, would consist of 800,000 shares of 500 francs each, issued at par.

Twenty-five francs would be paid on application, 100 francs on allotment, and the remainder would be called up as it became necessary, 5 per cent. being paid on the instalments until the completion of the work.

At last we have the public subscription asked for, and the American eagle aroused.

INTER-OCEANIC CANAL UNIVERSAL COMPANY, for cutting the American Isthmus, under the presidency and direction of M. Ferdinand de Lesseps, President-director of the Suez Canal. 800,000 shares of 500 francs each.

In pursuance of the bye-laws lodged with M. Champetier de Ribes, Notary in Paris, 10,000 shares are reserved for the Civil Society of original grantees, on account of the concession and surveys transferred by them to M. Ferdinand de Lesseps.

The remaining 790,000 shares are offered to the public for subscription.

The amount of each share is payable as follows:—25 francs on application, 100 francs on allotment.

The remaining 375 francs will be called up successively and according to the requirements of the undertaking, upon notice from the Council of Administration, published at least three months in advance.

Immediately after the constitution of the society steps will be taken for having the shares officially quoted.

After payment of 250 francs the shares may be converted into warrants to bearer by resolution of a general meeting.

Every proprietor of twenty shares is a member of general meetings.

An interest of 5 per cent. on the capital called will be paid to shareholders during the execution of the works.

The public subscription will be open, in Europe and in America, on Wednesday 6th and Thursday 7th of August.

The allotment of shares will be made in proportion to the total subscriptions, without distinction of nationality.

Subscriptions are received in Paris:—at the Suez Canal Universal Company, 9 Rue Clary; at the Comptoir d'Escompte, 14 Rue Bergère; at the Société Générale de Crédit Industriel et Commercial, No. 72 Rue de la Victoire; at the Société de Dépôts et de Comptes Courants, 2 Place de l'Opéra; at the Société Générale pour le Développement du Commerce et de l'Industrie en France, 54 Rue de Provence; at the Banque de Paris et des Pays-Bas, 3 Rue d'Antin; at the Crédit Lyonnais, 19 Boulevard des Italiens; at the Société Financière de Paris, 19 Rue Louis-le-Grand; at the Banque d'Escompte de Paris, 3 Rue Louis-le-Grand; and at their correspondents' in France and abroad.

Subscriptions may be sent in from this time by correspondence.

THE DARIEN CANAL.

Independently of the political contest in Congress, the most important proceeding of the session, in the popular view, was the introduction, in the closing days, of Senator Burnside's resolution, reaffirming the Monroe doctrine of American control on the American continent in reference to the proposed Darien Canal. The fact that the resolution was not acted upon is of no significance. It was intended simply as a notification, and the Foreign Committee will hereafter report it if the further development of the non-American portion of M. de Lesseps's scheme should make such a course necessary. Such a resolution would command a practically unanimous support whenever put to vote. The Monroe doctrine is a principle held as above all parties in the

United States, a cardinal doctrine of the national faith. Foreign control of
a Darien canal is as repugnant to American feelings as is foreign interference
with the road to India to an Englishman. There is a strong feeling deve-
loping on this subject, and the utterances of M. de Lesseps and his friends in
the Parisian newspapers do not allay it, though they are intended to do so,
and are faithfully telegraphed across the ocean. The canal project has begun
wrong, and it will not make any progress until the initial errors are corrected.
The selection of the route—which ignored all the practical surveys made by
Americans—offends our people. The proposal to guarantee the neutrality
of the canal is not enough. The Americans want the construction made by
an American route and under American auspices. The incorporation of the
company that has charge of the work must be American, to give the necessary
national control; and the assistance of all eminent French or other engineers
will be warmly welcomed. If M. de Lesseps concedes these things, and un-
does the initial errors, he may succeed; but I cannot imagine the shrewd
capitalists of the Old World investing in his enterprise under the present
unfavourable auspices to the enormous extent necessary for its completion.
The enterprise is looked upon in this country as practically a foreign interference in American affairs as marked as the ill-starred foreign occupation of
Mexico; and the United States, having no rebellion on its hands, can give,
and will give, undivided attention to the subject. Yet the Americans want
the canal constructed, provided it is done in our own way; and already there
are predictions that M. de Lesseps will abandon the peculiarly French auspices
under which he is now working, change his route to an American one, and
come over here and get an American charter for his company. I sincerely
hope he may. His great genius and limitless energy are the motive power
needed for a work of this kind. If he comes in, as did the Frenchmen of
old, under the American wing to help us, we will give him an enthusiastic
welcome. But he must recollect the cardinal doctrine that the American
continent is made for Americans, and that this rule applies as much to commercial enterprises as to governments. The canal must not only be neutral,
but its neutrality must be enforced by the American powers. The capital,
labour, and brains necessary to construct it may, and will probably, come
chiefly from Europe, but the work must be under American control. It will
be a work much similar to the existing Panama railroad. This railroad was
built under a charter granted by the Legislature of the State of New York,
its chief offices being in New York and its managers Americans; yet the
ownership of the line is largely held in England and Germany. The United
States Government not only maintains constant oversight of the railway,
sending naval vessels down there whenever the Central American disturb-
ances threaten it, but the Government will not allow any European Power
to interfere with it. This must be the rule with the Darien Canal, whenever
it is constructed. The American press has made very strong utterances on
this subject, and these views are universally held by all our public men and
by the Government as well as the people. I only repeat the prevalent senti-

ment. When M. de Lesseps turns his first sod on the Isthmus there will be a general inquiry as to what flag floats over the men who handle the spade. He is too sagacious not to select the right standard. At least this was the opinion of the well-informed correspondent of the 'Times' at the first announcement of the route selected.

Philadelphia, July 26.

Admiral Ammon, in reporting to the Government upon the proceedings of the Paris Inter-Oceanic Canal Congress, recommends the United States to form a commission of the ablest army engineers, inviting also the most eminent engineers of America and Europe, to meet and discuss the entire Canal question, unembarrassed by the rival personal interests attached to grants secured by French engineers.

The United States naval engineer Ménocal; who accompanied Admiral Ammon to Paris, also reports that the proceedings of the Paris Congress present the remarkable condition of engineers designing and estimating the cost of such an important work without a proper knowledge of the ground on which the works are to be constructed, which was generally regarded, as well as the cost, to be a matter for after-consideration.

July 27.

It is announced in New York that subscriptions will be opened on August 6 for the stock in M. de Lesseps's Darien Canal Company. The American view and criticism of the auspices under which the company starts, as also of the route proposed, are so unfavourable that it is believed the American subscriptions will be comparatively small.

Philadelphia, July 31.

The Government has furnished for publication an abstract of Admiral Ammon's report on the Paris Inter-Oceanic Canal Congress, wherein Admiral Ammon declares that the Congress from its first sitting had within it two parties of speculators, one advocating the Nicaragua and the other the Panama route; that the latter has been carried through the Congress notwithstanding the irrefragable proof of the impracticability of the route, through a system of appointing delegates; that able engineers generally favoured the Nicaragua route; that the proposed *canal à niveau* by the Isthmus of Panama, either with or without a tunnel, has been shown to be hopelessly impracticable if considered as a commercial question; and he recommends the calling of another congress of competent engineers to consider the question. The report is stronger than the earlier statements, some of which I telegraphed you. It would appear that while Washington advices are that Admiral Ammon's course is fully approved by the Government, and also by letters received from many influential men throughout the country, the American Press strongly sustain Admiral Ammon; and the wide-spread belief of the impracticability of the Panama route, with possible political complications hereafter with the United States Government, indicate that no American capitalist will invest in the scheme under present auspices. The Crédit Lyonnais has a branch office in New York opened for stock subscrip-

tions, while news telegrams from Paris represent M. de Lesseps as saying at Bordeaux that American support has been secured for the Darien project. Diligent inquiry in this country fails to confirm this statement. Most of the leading American journals to-day discuss the subject, advocating the proposal to call another congress of experienced engineers under the auspices of the United States. The ' New York Tribune ' says that some other route might be found better, cheaper, and safer than that by Panama ; and, while American sentiment favours the undertaking, it is in no spirit of opposition that American engineers declare the Panama route has fatal defects, and that more time should be taken for examination of the plans. They speak because they happen to know, and wish to prevent the commission of a colossal blunder. The ' New York World ' says that it may be taken for granted, from the point of view of politics, that the American people will not look quietly upon the building up of a foreign proprietary power astride the vital line of connexion between the Atlantic and Pacific domains of the Republic. The ' New York Times ' says it is hardly possible, in the face of the demonstrated impossibility of securing navigable waters at the ocean level by the Panama route, that any thing like the required amount of subscriptions can be obtained. The certainty of distrust by American capitalists and the opposition by the United States Government will go far to kill the scheme to which M. de Lesseps has so rashly lent the weight of his name. The ' Philadelphia Public Ledger ' says it is becoming well understood that the Panama Canal scheme was adopted by a selected, not to say packed, Paris Congress, and can meet with little favour in this country, because the choice of the route was controlled by personal speculative considerations, and not made because of engineering or commercial advantages, there never having been a survey, in an engineering sense, of the Panama route in view of the construction of the canal. Therefore there can be no trustworthy estimate of the cost of the scheme, contrary to the judgment of all the American engineers acquainted with the country where the prospectus locates the proposed canal. The ocean-level of the canal there is regarded as utterly impracticable. The attempt failing, as it must do, after large amounts of capital have been sunk in it, must have the effect of postponing indefinitely the construction of a canal on a practical route such as is proposed by Lake Nicaragua. The ' Ledger ' recommends a reexamination of the subject by a conference of skilled engineers.

Washington, Aug. 3.

Mr. Ménocal, civil engineer, with the approval of the Secretary of the Navy, and by invitation of the Nicaraguan Government, will shortly leave to complete, under the auspices of the above Government, the work on the unfinished portions of the survey of the Nicaraguan route for the proposed Inter-Oceanic Canal.

' The Builder,' August 2, 1879, has the following :—

" *The New Canal.*

" Thanks to the active energy of M. de Lesseps, not a day has been lost since the meeting of the Paris Geographical Congress some weeks back, which determined the question and many of the details of the Panama Canal, which is to separate the two Americas. M. de Lesseps has within a few days visited, in company with Mr. Appleton, a number of French cities, in each of which an enthusiastic welcome has been given to the projector of the Suez Canal, who has now come forward as so active a promoter of the new American canal, which he promises the engineering world will be completed before six years' time. On the 14th inst. M. de Lesseps was received by the Geographical Society of Rouen, and the lecture delivered by the eminent engineer was more than once interrupted by the enthusiastic applause of the large assembly. M. de Lesseps happily possesses the power of expressing his thoughts ably and with facility ; his style is simple, and, above all, his statements are set forth with a clearness and confidence that leave no room for doubt. It is to this fact that is due the immense popularity of M. de Lesseps and the confidence with which his predictions are accepted.

" The enterprise is to commence very shortly, the Scientific Congress having agreed that in the first week in August a subscription is to be opened. The Commission has estimated the maximum of the expense at a milliard of francs (40 millions sterling), and 36,000 workmen are to be employed during the five or six years that the work lasts. Fortunately, as M. de Lesseps gracefully remarked at Rouen, the piercing of the Isthmus of Panama will not be so difficult as that of the Isthmus of Suez, owing to the bonds of friendship and the recollections of old brotherhood that exist between France and America ; and it is, doubtless, as a compliment to that country that M. de Lesseps's little daughter, a child of six years of age, will, by means of electricity, demolish the first obstacle of the Isthmus, as did, if we remember rightly, the daughter of President Hayes, the famous passage of Hell Gate, near New York.

" It may be imagined, in the midst of what applause M. de Lesseps announced in his speech at Rouen a few days back, that he invited the company present to meet him again three years' hence, on the day of the first voyage by a French punt through the new canal. Every thing augurs for the best in the new enterprise, which it may be imagined M. de Lesseps would earnestly desire to see terminated ; indeed his admirers express such hope in his energy, that they openly announced the only possibility of his succumbing, when some further project—perhaps the opening up of the great African continent, in which he takes so active an interest—shall have completed the trio of the noble enterprises of a life devoted so generously for the benefit of future generations.

" But M. de Lesseps is not the only aged enthusiast in France who has aided by his powerful influence the work of the new canal, so typical an

enterprise of this teeming century. At a recent solemn masonic meeting of the French and Scotch lodge, Clemente Amitié, held in Paris on the occasion of the fourth anniversary of the initiation of Mr. Littré, the illustrious Academician, a meeting, honoured by the presence, among many other notabilities, of M. Gambetta, M. Ferry, and M. de Lesseps, M. Littré, prevented by illness from attending the ceremony, addressed to his ' brothers ' a letter of excuse, not alone expressing a formal regret, but containing a glowing glorification of modern industry, and particularly of the great enterprise of the piercing of the Isthmus of Panama.

" ' What was but the other day,' as the veteran Academician remarked, ' but a bold initiative, a mere projected scheme, became a hope when the learned explorers to whom was entrusted the duty of studying the circumstances and conditions of the several projects put forward, returned, not without, however, more than one valuable life having been sacrificed in the dangerous exploration ; and now the project is almost realized. The plans are accepted, the financial combinations have already commenced, and soon will be struck the first blows which will unite two oceans, by means of an enterprise, one of the glories of the close of the nineteenth century, a great project, simple in its conception, laborious in its execution, beneficial for ever in its results.

" ' Christopher Columbus, adventuring into the unknown immensity of the Atlantic, believed by that road to gain the East Indies, but his advance was barred by the long stretch of the Americas, from pole to pole, with their narrow strip of land connecting the two halves, and effectually opposing a barrier to further progress westwards.

" ' But the man of modern times can no longer hear the sound of the waves of two oceans beating on shores so near and yet so far separated, without his active intelligence imagining in what manner the obstacles may be cut through. To conceive and carry out enterprises of such magnitude, savants, geologists, and engineers, aided by all the powerful army of modern machinery and immense capital, are absolutely necessary.

" ' Science and industry, in concert, undertake to change, in a given place, the system of the terrestrial globe. The man of the present day brings unhesitatingly to bear his active hand, and, turning the sense of a fine Latin verse, he has the right to believe himself engendered for the whole human race (*toti genitum se credere mundo*), to feel himself capable of embracing the whole system of his home, and modify it according to his views and profit.

" ' When the first Montgolfière rose into the air in Paris, in the presence of an astonished crowd, an old lady of quality cried, ' They will discover when I am dead the secret of avoiding death.' That secret has not been found ; but modern science has advanced, and daily advances more rapidly into the workshop of nature and her processes, and extracts from it powers which multiply indefinitely the means at our disposal, so insignificant in our origin, so potent in the present day.

" ' Society becomes each year richer, and each year presents itself to the

thoughtful as a growing difficulty, the best employment of these riches. In the international disorder in which at present is plunged so many nations of the world, when it would be desirable that the real benefits, such as we possess, should not be compromised lightly, every thing which serves to shackle selfish or ill-regulated impulses in rulers, or in people, should be looked upon with satisfaction; and nothing gives greater promise to the needs of security than these gigantic and cosmopolitan enterprises, which, appealing to the world at large, render the community a service that is incalculable.

"'Recognized as powers which must be taken into consideration, they establish beneficial neutralities which circumscribe the battle-fields of the world, and impose limits on the spread of their terrible destruction. It would almost seem as if the genius of the present hour had deliberately placed in contrast the double spectacle of the great wars and great enterprises of which we are now witnesses, like the Jupiter of the Iliad seizing his golden scales to weigh the destinies of the heroes, as if that genius had taken its shining scales to weigh out before the world the work of conquest and of labour.

"'But the other day the cannon roared along the Balkans; for religion, for panslavism, for aggrandizement, Russia had drawn her sword, and, after her victory, Russia binds up her wounds and looks hopefully forward to the day when they will be cicatrized.

"'And now an expedition is being prepared resolutely to attack the Isthmus of Panama. Whatever may be the unforeseen difficulties and obstacles met with, we may rest assured that they will be overcome; and commerce will avail itself of a now highway, which nature had till now refused it, and increasing prosperity will follow in this great track traced by our engineers. Must we be astonished if the genius of the hour shows with pride the two scales of its golden balance?'

"This warm and glowing letter of M. Littré has met in France with universal applause, and cannot fail in other countries than his own to supply ample matter for the consideration of the thoughtful. It is in this particular that such noble and durable enterprises, of interest to the world at large, deserve so much more consideration than is at present given to them, and in which they are so often set aside for pettier and more selfish aims. It has with reason been remarked that the future lies in the hands of the engineer, and each day tends more to prove the truth of this fact in the interest we are called upon to devote to the examination of fresh projects which but a quarter of a century since seemed of apparently impossible completion. It is for the Governments of the world, instead of shackling the international action of the thoughtful and the practical, whose common patriotism consists in the advance of intelligence and prosperity for the world at large, to aid each other in this great work which it is the duty of each of us individually to help on and remit as worthy trustees to future generations."

That nothing should be wanting to ensure the success of the issue of shares, especially among the *ouvriers*, the *bourgeoisie*, and the peasants (the latter of whom, according to Prince Jerome Napoleon, are sincerely attached to their "*clocher*"), it was necessary to anticipate a spiritual as well as a temporal prestige for the undertaking, and accordingly we find the following telegram from Rome, Aug. 6 :—" The Pope to-day, after the details of the proposed Panama Canal scheme had been explained to him by the engineer, Signor Gioja, pronounced a blessing upon the work, and expressed the hope that it might prove, morally even more than materially, a bond of union between the Old and the New Worlds."

This moral view of an engineering problem, however, seems to have had little influence across the Atlantic, for we learn from Philadelphia (Aug. 6) that, " at the request of the Nicaraguan Government, negotiation shave been renewed by the United States concerning the inter-oceanic canal route, the United States taking great interest in the Nicaraguan route and recent agitation reviving Nicaragua's interest on the subject. At the instance of Nicaragua, this Government has given Engineer Ménocal, who was at the Paris Congress, permission to visit Nicaragua in the autumn to complete the unfinished surveys. The Government appears also decided upon active operations to thwart the Panama scheme under its present auspices. Should any work be attempted, which is doubtful, the Secretary of the Navy has directed the Commander of the United States Squadron in the Gulf of Mexico to maintain a close surveillance along the Central American coasts, promptly checking any attempt to interfere with the interests of the United States."

(Aug. 7.) " The opposition to the Darien Canal scheme in the United States has had the anticipated effect of checking American stock subscriptions to the enterprise. The Credit Lyonnais agency in New York opened subscriptions on Wednesday. Five hundred shares have been taken, and the agent is of opinion that probably he will get 200 more by the time the subscription closes. To-night few subscribe, all being personal friends of M. de Lesseps."

(Aug. 8.) " The aggregate subscriptions in the United States to the Inter-Oceanic Canal Company amounted to about 600 shares."

(Aug. 9.) " According to the *Cote Européenne*, an opponent of M. de Lesseps's Panama Canal scheme, only 160,000 shares were subscribed in Paris up to yesterday evening, when the subscription was closed. The number of shares offered in the prospectus was 800,000. The exact figures will, no doubt, be known very shortly."

Finally, as is always the case, it is all the fault of perfidious Albion; as M. de Lesseps, speaking at Beauvais a few days ago on the Panama Canal, and contending that the Monroe doctrine had nothing to do with it, told the following anecdote :—" In 1855, when the Anglo-French alliance had reached the culminating point, Queen Victoria came to Paris. Do you know what was the first thing Her Majesty said to the Emperor when she had an oppor-

tunity of talking seriously with him? You could never imagine. She asked him immediately to have a stop put to the Suez Canal works. The Emperor twisted his long moustache and replied that he had heard of M. de Lesseps, but that he was not personally acquainted with him, and that it was impossible to prevent him from continuing his work; that if he had gone and asked Queen Victoria to interfere with the work of any English contractor he would in all probability have been ill received. The conversation was not continued. Thus it was that the ill-will of England with regard to a canal she now considers so precious remained without effect. There are in America extremely energetic Latin races who take the greatest interest in the Panama Canal. People are much mistaken if they fancy that these peoples would remain indifferent in the event of a hostile or malevolent attitude on the part of North America. I have proofs to the contrary, and I know that the United States do not think of offering resistance, which would expose them to the censure of the whole southern population of the New World."

The following letter has lately appeared :—

Upon the revival of the Interoceanic Canal project, discussed at the Paris Congress in May last, I felt that it would be churlish indeed to abstain from rendering any assistance in my power towards the furtherance of such a project; but, as my medical adviser peremptorily placed his veto against my going there myself, I sent over a confidential representative, in whom I had confidence, to offer, on my behalf, any advice and assistance in furtherance of the object in view.

Before I proceed to point out the steps which, in my judgment, should be taken to secure the prompt and economic execution of the work, I hope it will not be considered egotistical if I quote one or two paragraphs of my address to the Congress, to show how deeply I am interested in the matter from long practical experience and participation in transit projects on the spot.

The following concluding passages of that address refer to this part of the subject :—

" It is right, however, that I should indicate the range of my experience, and I may say that between the years 1845 and 1851 I was engaged, ' on and off,' on the surveys of the coast line of the Pacific Ocean, from Cape Corrientes to the port of Realejo, especially in and around the Bay of Panama —a coast line of about 1000 miles, my attention being particularly directed to the Gulf of San Miguel, the approaches of the Nippi and to the Chepo, or Bayano river, a route having the recommendation of possessing a waterway approaching the Atlantic Ocean nearer than any other, besides passing through large estates also with a right of way to the Atlantic, belonging to the Central American Association, of which I have had the honour to be chairman for more than twelve years.

" I should mention that my Association is equally anxious with myself to

b

further by any means in its power the grand object of the meeting, and on the last Board day passed a resolution to that effect.

"On the Atlantic coast I have had an equal, if not more extensive, experience.

"Between 1859 and 1861 I was stationed as senior naval officer between Cape Gracios a Dios and Colon or Aspinwall, and since that time I have often crossed Central America. I have been no less than six times through Nicaragua, obtaining an accurate section with the theodolite between the Atlantic and the Lake of Nicaragua, on a line parallel to and about 40 miles distant from the river San Juan.

"I have pointed out fully in my works, 'The Gate of the Pacific,' 1863, and 'Dottings by the Roadside, 1869,' and this meeting is of course aware, that there are still other routes to the northward, such as Tehuantepec and Honduras, for which latter I was for some time Special Commissioner, and for more than a year devoted my best attention towards completing the Interoceanic Railway; but circumstances over which I had no control prevented me from achieving that object. I am bound to say, however, that I still have faith in it, and believe that the Government of the country would satisfy the just claims of their creditors to the last franc, if only those creditors would bring a gentle pressure to bear on their debtor, and insist upon payment, if not in money then in land, in exchange for their bonds.

"Bedford Pim."

The result of the meeting at Paris has been the adoption of a route for the Canal on a parallel line with the Panama Railway from Limon Bay on the Atlantic to Panama Bay on the Pacific; a selection unfortunate for many reasons, and not the least is that, unhappily, there seems already to have arisen a strong element of disapproval in the United States which, at a time when unity of action on all sides is of essential importance, is much to be deplored.

The French, under the able leadership of M. de Lesseps, have chosen the above route, and, doubtless, will spare no pains to accomplish their object; but they unquestionably have been hurried in this adoption, and, it is to be feared, will repent at leisure.

The assertion is boldly made, and it has a large amount of truth in it, that nothing is too gigantic and difficult for M. de Lesseps to overcome.

The Suez Canal, it is said, is an accomplished fact; and with such an achievement emblazoned on his banner there can be no halting on the part of the followers of M. de Lesseps in the presence of any amount of engineering difficulties.

The enthusiasm of his countrymen is not only excusable, it is praiseworthy; but the difference between the two isthmuses in every single attribute never seems to have called for a moment's consideration, much less do the French seem to have thought that the work of the Suez Canal was child's play as compared to that which will have to be overcome at Panama.

In page 16 of 'The Gate of the Pacific' these words occur:—

" It is hardly possible to conceive any thing more widely different than the nature of the connecting links joining together the continents of the Old and New World. In the former we have a broad, flat, low expanse of parched and arid country, rather more than 70 miles across, a complete desert; in the latter a mountainous surface and very irregular coast-line, extending over many hundreds of miles, teeming with animal and vegetable life, and only at its narrowest part about half the width of the Old-World isthmus. There is another striking dissimilarity—the one possessing the earliest records of the human race in readable hieroglyphics, and crowded with historical associations of the deepest interest to mankind, whilst the other is a comparatively modern addition to the history of the world, with writings still an enigma to science."

Without in any way attempting to detract from M. de Lesseps's well earned reputation, I may add to the above that which I have learned by practical acquaintance with both the Isthmus of Suez and the Isthmus of Central America, namely, that M. de Lesseps will find the nature of the task he has now set himself to accomplish very different from the one he has lately completed. Unlike Suez, he will find that there is no forced labour to hand, no such sympathy as he found in Egypt, in Turkey, and in France; no similarity of climate, no powerful connexions to assist him with their influence; but, on the contrary, a great shadow overhanging him at every step he takes : I mean the "Monroe Doctrine, America for the Americans,"—a sentiment he will find as deeply impressed in the breasts of the people of the United States as any sentiment ever interwoven with the national life of a European country, a sentiment, moreover, with which no one can find fault, and, what is more, against which it will be perfectly useless to contend.

The above are only some of the difficulties which he will have to contend with, and not one of which can be put lightly aside.

It is not my purpose to go into details as to which is the best route. This has been done in the very ablest manner by my friend Captain Maury, whose name is a household word all over the globe. In a letter dated July 1866, addressed to me, he goes fully into the subject; and as every word falling from this distinguished physical geographer carries great and deserved weight with it, I shall make no apology for the following copious extract[a] from his letter :—

" 30 Harley Street, Cavendish Square, London,
July 1866.

" MY DEAR CAPTAIN PIM,—I had occasion some years ago to study, more or less closely, almost every route between the British possessions on the north and the Isthmus of Darien on the south, whether for rail or for canal, that had up to that time been attempted or projected across the American continent.

" Owing to the character of the researches with which I have been for more than twenty years engaged, my attention was directed to those routes rather

in their physical and commercial aspects than to their topographical features or to their facilities of construction.

"The great importance of one or more *good* commercial highways across Central America being admitted, the whole question as to route resolves itself pretty much into a question of the cost of construction and the facility of ingress and egress by sea to and from the opposite termini; the latter is an affair of winds and currents: their influence is powerful. Panama has the advantage of land transit; Nicaragua has the advantage in winds, terminal ports, and climate. The first is obvious; but to place the latter in a clear light, a little explanation may be necessary.

   *   *   *   *   *   *

"I have spoken of a calm belt about the equator; Panama is within its range. Owing to the contour of the Central American isthmus, the height and direction of the mountain-ranges by which it is traversed, and the influence of these upon winds, this calm belt is greatly enlarged on the Pacific or lee side of the isthmus.

"It is difficult to convey to one who has never experienced these calms an idea of the obstinacy with which they vex navigation. We are all familiar with calms at sea which last for a few hours, or even a day: but here they last for days and weeks at a time. I have known vessels going to or from Panama to be detained by them for months at a time.

   *   *   *   *   *   *

"On one occasion the British Admiralty, wishing to send one of their sailing vessels into the Arctic Ocean from Panama in time to save the season, had her towed by a steamer through this calm belt, and carried 700 miles out to sea before she could find a breeze.

   *   *   *   *   *   *

"These remarks apply to the approach and departure by sea to or from the Pacific terminus of any route across the Isthmus of Panama or Darien, and even with greater force to the Atrato and others on the South-American side of Panama.

"In short, the results of my investigation into the winds and currents of the sea, and their influence upon the routes of commerce, authorize the opinion which I have expressed before, and which I here repeat, namely, if Nature by one of her convulsions should rend the continent of America in twain and make a channel across the Isthmus of Panama or Darien as deep, and as wide, and as free as the Straits of Dover, it would never become a commercial thoroughfare for sailing-vessels, saving the outward-bound and those that could reach it with leading winds. Steamers would, and coasters might, use it; but homeward-bound vessels in the China, India, or Australian trade, rarely.

   *   *   *   *   *   *

"We come now to the Nicaraguan routes: of these there are several. Though longer across from ocean to ocean than Panama, some of them have already, and with a degree of success by no means discouraging, competed with it before the world for public favour.

   *   *   *   *   *   *

" Skilful engineers, both French and American, have examined them [the engineering difficulties and topographical features of this Nicaraguan route]. Those of both nations report gradients gentle enough for a canal. In truth, the lakes, their distance from the sea, and their height above it, indicate that the summit-level is to be attained without any very steep ascents.

" It is to this part of the Isthmus, too, to which we must look for a route which shall best fulfil the present requirements of commerce between the two oceans, as well as of transportation and travel between the Pacific shores of North America on the one hand, and the Atlantic shores (both of Europe and America) on the other.

*   *   *   *   *   *

" Vessels under canvas would, in the main, do the fetching and carrying for the Nicaragua route, which (for reasons already stated) cannot be done for Panama. The aggregate amount of this trade is immense, and it is neither accommodated for Panama, nor Panama for it.

*   *   *   *   *   *

" Therefore, returning again to the physical features of the Panama route, as I promised to do, we can now compare more in detail than I have yet done the advantages possessed by each, as far as those advantages are influenced by facilities of navigation, by the elements, by salubrity of climate, and by the dictates of commerce.

" The French and English Admiralty Charts give the most accurate information that I possess concerning the harbours at the opposite ends of the two routes, Panama and Nicaragua—I mean as to mere anchoring-ground, depth of water, and shelter afforded.

" It is proper to remark here, that I was a great friend, an earnest advocate, and an active supporter of the Panama road, giving it in 1849 the preference over all other Isthmian routes. At that time my ' wind and current' investigations had not extended into the Pacific Ocean; and the discovery of those causes which make the approach and departure to and from the Bay of Panama so very difficult for sailing-vessels, had not been sufficiently established to give them their proper weight.

*   *   *   *   *   *

" You will observe at a glance that the Isthmus of Panama or Darien is, on account of these winds and calms, in a purely commercial point of view, the most out of the way place of any part of the Pacific coast of intertropical America.

*   *   *   *   *   *

" ' Lieut. Maury,' remarks Mr. Hull, master of H.M.S. ' Havannah,' ' truly says that the passage under canvas from Panama to California is one of the most tedious, uncertain, and vexatious that is known to navigators.'

" Realejo (Nicaragua) is in the northern verge of these calms (Panama), and where they have nearly ceased to be vexatious to the navigator any season. Here, then, is the physical advantage in favour of the Nicaraguan route for which it is difficult to find the money-value.

*   *   *   *   *   *

"The transit route of Nicaragua is exempt from these heavy drawbacks of dampness and disease. It passes through a salubrious climate. The soil is productive; its pastures abound in cattle. I never heard of any disease peculiar to the country, nor of especial virulence there.

"(Signed)   M. F. MAURY."

I do not care to make a single comment on my distinguished friend's letter, his facts speak more eloquently than any words of mine. I am very sorry to throw the smallest discouragement upon the enterprise of M. de Lesseps; but, looking to the international importance of the subject, I could not possibly keep to myself the views of my friend Captain Maury—views which, as a practical man well acquainted with those parts of the world, I have no alternative but to indorse.

While fully recognizing the great abilities and reputation of M. de Lesseps; I am strongly of opinion that the gigantic enterprise he has undertaken, beside which the Suez Canal dwarfs to a stagnant ditch, should not be left on the shoulders of one man; indeed cannot be left with any one person, however powerful, without entailing certain loss and disappointment.

The canalization of the Isthmus of Central America, at a point where not only steamers but sailing-vessels can use it, is a work for nations, and can only be undertaken and successfully completed by an international combination. A guarantee of one per cent. on the required capital by England, France, and America would doubtless secure the necessary money, while a shallow canal to begin with, say eight feet in depth, with the vessels lifted on pontoons (as in the Victoria Docks), and conveyed from ocean to ocean in that manner, would amply suffice for the present commercial wants, and would, moreover, not require even one half of the colossal sums at which the cost of the Panama Canal is at present estimated.

There are other points of vast importance which should be fully discussed and settled before beginning work; but I have already so transgressed the limits of a letter that nothing but the importance of the subject can be urged in excuse.

(Signed)   BEDFORD PIM,
            Captain R.N., M.P.

2 Crown Office Row, Temple,
    London, E.C.

THE NICARAGUAN RAILWAY.

"The narrow neck of land which connects the two great continents of America, and appears so insignificant a strip on maps of the world, remains to this day a country but little known. Covered for the greater part with dense virgin forests, having a hot and humid climate, in some parts highly detrimental to the health of Europeans, and thinly inhabited by tribes of Indians, many of whom proudly boast of never having been conquered by the white man, the great American isthmus opposes such an effectual barrier to rapid and close intercourse between the Atlantic and Pacific, that although several centuries have elapsed since it was discovered, we have *till*

now only two practicable highways across it, along which European settlements have been established, those of Panama and Nicaragua. No sooner does the traveller leave these highways than he finds himself face to face with all the difficulties, dangers, and privations which were encountered by Balboa when first he pushed his way to the South Sea. Indeed, so little have things changed since then, that the latest narratives of Central American explorations (as detailed by Mr. Collinson at the last Meeting of the Geographical Society) read but like a paraphrase of that of the ill-fated Spanish discoverer.

"Our readers are aware that some years ago Captain Bedford Pim, R.N., demonstrated that a railroad made across Nicaragua would enjoy great advantages over that of Panama by having good ports at the termini, passing through a salubrious country, shortening the distance between England and some of her most important possessions, and, as a matter of course, being a cheaper route. Naturally enough, the scheme was violently objected to; and the gallant Captain had to visit Nicaragua over and over again in order to meet all the objections which could possibly be urged against it. During these visits he became acquainted with a new gold region; and this led to the acquisition of the Javali and other valuable Chontales mines by American and English capitalists. Sir Roderick Murchison has gratefully acknowledged the great service Captain Pim has rendered to geographical science, not only by his own personal exertions and zeal, but by associating with himself men like Messrs. Seemann, Collinson, and Oliver, who, under his guidance, penetrated Nicaragua in various directions, and accumulated much solid geographical knowledge. The singular persistency with which Captain Pim had stuck, through good report and through evil report, to his resolve of demonstrating beyond the possibility of a doubt the practicability of connecting the Atlantic and Pacific by means of a railroad through Nicaragua has now been triumphantly proved by Mr. Collinson carrying a spirit-level right through the thick primeval forests which stretch from the Lake of Nicaragua to the Atlantic seaboard.

"It must have been gratifying to Captain Pim when, pushing up the Rama river, he effected a junction with Mr. Collinson's party, and found that he then possessed all the proof required to convince even the most sceptical that the Atlantic and Pacific oceans can be connected by means of a railroad across Nicaragua. It must have forcibly reminded him of the moment when, after travelling for days over the dreary snow-fields of the arctic region, he reached H.M.S. 'Investigator,' and thus closed, as Humboldt graphically expressed it, by a scene highly dramatic, the great tragedy of the North-west Passage."—*From* 'THE GLOBE,' *November 28, 1867.*

With a view to assist Captain Pim, R.N., in an examination of the route proposed by him for a railway across the isthmus, I started for Central America in January 1867. Following is my diary of rough notes made

en route; but first I should briefly allude to the physical geography of the country immediately surrounding the Nicaraguan lakes.

Three lines of mountains, nearly parallel to the coast of the Pacific, pass through Nicaragua. The first ridge to the north is, strictly speaking, more the edge of a tableland than a chain of mountains, the tablelands sloping to the east and north-east. These include the high mountains of New Segovia and the Alto Grande in the Chontales district. Diminishing in elevation towards the south-east, they slope to the San Juan, where the country is generally flat and swampy.

The watershed between the Pacific and Atlantic oceans forms a second range close to and following the coast-line of the Pacific, connecting the famous volcano of Conseguina, at the entrance of the Gulf of Fonseca, with the lofty volcanic peaks of Costa Rica; it has occasional depressions most suitable for easy communication between the ocean and the lakes.

Between these two lines of elevation, which form the sides of an elongated basin or valley containing the Nicaraguan lakes, there is a third line of isolated volcanic cones; these form a characteristic feature in the scenery of Nicaragua.

These commence from the Maribios on the north-west, including Mount Viego, the Peaks of Santa Clara, Telica, Orota, Las Pilas, Axosco, to Momotombo, the last mentioned the highest mountain in Nicaragua, an active volcano, reaching an elevation of 7000 feet.

This line is continued by the peak of Momotombita, in the Lake of Managua, the peaks of Chiltepee forming the peninsula north of Managua, followed by Masaya, Monbacho, Zapatero, Ometepee, Madera, and Solentinamo, these four latter forming the conspicuous islands in the large Lake of Nicaragua.

The lake of Managua, thirty-five miles, and Nicaragua, ninety miles in length, have respectively an elevation of 156·11 feet and 128·3 feet above the oceans. They are connected by the Estero Panaloya, twenty-five miles, in which the Cascade of Tipitapa, with a fall of 13 feet, prevents the free communication between them. This lake-system is drained at the south-east by the San Juan, which runs in a tortuous course of ninty-three miles to the Atlantic.

Mr. Osbert Salvin, the ornithologist, has, from long studying the peculiarities of the Central-American bird-fauna, come to the conclusion that an oceanic separation is indicated as having formerly existed between Costa Rica and the country north of the Nicaraguan lakes, a strait existing where the lakes now stand. Conclusive natural evidence proves that centuries ago the sea covered the entire space now occupied by the mouths and swampy deltas of the San Juan; while among the historical accounts of the country are distinct records of the time in old Spain's palmy days, when her ships of war regularly sailed up the river and across the lake to Granada. Now a shallow canoe steered and paddled by dexterous Caribs can hardly clear, on the crest of the wave, without touching the bar; and light river-steamers with stern-wheels and drawing, when laden, only 10 inches of water,

can scarcely grope their way from rapid to rapid, whose rocky bottoms, strewn with boulders, and rapidly flowing current effectually bar their further passage.

Every year it becomes more evident to all living on its banks or using its stream that the flow of water is becoming less in the San Juan ; and even the least observant native dwelling on the lake will tell how its banks are rising year by year visibly before his eyes ; how the river Panaloya connecting the two great lakes is becoming drier every season, so much so that at times lately no water-connexion has existed between them. Noting the fact that these lakes are in the middle of the great volcanic range bisecting the isthmus which dies out to nothing before reaching the low alluvial shores of the Atlantic, may it not be conjectured that the gradual upheaval of the centre, while the coast has remained almost unmoved, should year by year increase the gradients of the river, and by creating a more rapid flow of waters cause the perceptible drainage of the lakes and lower the level of the waters ? Also will not this help to account for the formation of the deltas and the silting up of the estuary of the San Juan ?

Formerly the river must have flowed out calmly almost on a level from lake to ocean ; whilst now the turbid waters, hurrying down with ever in-creasing velocity, carry with them the *débris* disturbed by the floods of the rainy season till suddenly they find a level bed, and, from the resistance of the denser sea-water with the frequent violent " northers " of these latitudes blowing full upon them, they are arrested in their course and deposit the suspended material.

To the east of the lakes and north of the San Juan, along the whole of the disputed frontiers of Mosquito, is an almost *terra incognita*, occu-pied by vast impenetrable forests of gigantic trees, dense underwood, and the trees matted with entangled vines and creepers. But few Indians, and those fast disappearing, live on the banks of the rivers which drain this country. The Spaniard Americans never penetrate far from their savannahs on the lake, with the exception of a few hardy india-rubber hunters, who venture up the small creeks, but seldom wander far from their canoes. Such was the country I had to explore. This was twelve years ago ; since then, however, affairs have improved, for we learn there is a prospect of direct steam communication being permanently established between the Atlantic and Lake Nicaragua. Already the passage of the river San Juan has been forced by the steamer ' Coburg '; and the Government of the Republic of Nicaragua has engaged the services of an engineer to remove the principal obstacles to the progress of large steamers up and down the river, or to con-struct a canal, if necessary, by which the rapids may be avoided. At the same time, railway-communication between the lake, the interior, and the Atlantic coast is being rapidly extended. It is proposed to construct a new railway between Corinto, the new port on the Atlantic, Chinandega, Leon, and the Pacific shore. The first section from Corinto to Chinandega will be

completed as early as possible, in order to test the capacity of the country to bear the extension of the line right across the isthmus. It is anticipated that the undertaking will prove highly successful. The trade of Corinto is rapidly increasing, the exports of cocoa, sugar, cedar-wood, and especially of coffee being of considerable value.

The last news as regards the Panama scheme, up to the date of going to press, is extracted from the 'Standard':—

"There are not many men more deservedly popular than M. Ferdinand de Lesseps, and the disappointment he has experienced in his attempt at forming a Company for cutting through the Isthmus of Panama meets with general sympathy. But M. de Lesseps is not discouraged; and although the public have not responded to his appeal, he means to go on with the scheme. Faith removes mountains, and therefore it may be taken for granted that perseverance and energy will enable M. de Lesseps to collect the money required to make a ship canal between the Atlantic and Pacific. He has issued the following circular, which speaks for itself:—

"'The issue of 800,000 shares, which took place on the 6th and 7th instant in Europe and America, has not been taken up. In accordance with clause 82 of the statutes of the Interoceanic Canal Company, I might call a general meeting of the subscribers, and, with their cooperation, form a universal company for the piercing of the American isthmus; but, feeling confident of ultimate success, I shall wait until light shall have been thrown on the attacks directed against our work at the last hour, with a view to check the favourable impulse which had shown itself at first. The arguments of our opponents may be thus summed up. On the one hand they have exaggerated the expenditure and underrated the receipts, with a view to show that though the opening of a new maritime pathway to commerce and civilization was a good one in a business point of view, it was not likely to pay. On the other hand, it has been attempted to show that the scheme would fail through the hostility of the United States of North America. To the first argument the able contractor who removed the bar of El Ghizeh in the Suez Canal has undertaken to reply. M. Couvoux and his associates, to whom is due the great works for the regular flow of the Danube and the enlargement of the port of Antwerp, are about to undertake, at their own expense, a fresh survey, with a view to the execution of the Interoceanic Canal. They have made up their minds to undertake the work either by contract or at their own risk at my choice, and will permit no doubt to subsist as to the receipts showing a surplus over the expenditure. As to the second objection, I shall myself deal with it in a trip I am about to take to the United States. It is only on my return that I shall constitute the Universal Company in virtue of the important and liberal concession conceded by the independent Government of the United States of Columbia.

The subscribers who in Europe and America have responded to my appeal by paying up 55 francs per share can, from this date, have their money returned. No deduction will be made. They will receive scrip which, on the formation of the Company, entitles them to the number of shares they applied for without reduction. The money left unclaimed will be lodged at the Bank of France. A half-monthly bulletin, the first number to appear on September 1, will keep the founders of, and subscribers to, the Canal informed of all that concerns them during the preliminary works.'

" M. de Lesseps is a frank and straightforward man, as the above letter shows; but one objection to his canal scheme he has not dealt with, namely, the pestiferous climate of the region through which the canal has to be cut. The next great objection is the hostility of the United States. To England, no doubt, the canal would be a boon, as affording a short cut to Australia and New Zealand, some of the Chinese ports and Japan; but the United States have nothing to gain by it, and, once it existed, it would interfere very materially with the railway traffic between New York and San Francisco. He thinks that he can talk the Americans out of their hostility to the canal. I have no doubt he will be received enthusiastically by our Transatlantic kinsmen, who appreciate pluck and enterprise; but they have a keen eye to their own interests, and unless he can persuade them to undertake themselves the construction of the canal, it is not improbable that the shortest way to Australia will continue to be that other creation of M. de Lesseps, the Suez Canal."—*21st August,* 1879.

I will now commence my diary.

S. P. O.,

Scientific Club,

September 4th, 1879.   4 Savile Row. W.

RAFT VOYAGE DOWN THE RIVER RAMA,
MOSQUITO TERRITORY.

OFF DUTY.

RAMBLES OF A GUNNER.

Buckingham Villas, Brockhurst, near Gosport.
January 15, 1867.

Frost continues. Shave for last time. Stay at home until 11 A.M., when the gunsmith arrives with ammunition, &c., powder in portable magazine, and last, but not least, the bill. Galt's man follows, with clothes &c.; and my packing is nearly finished. Fill the chest, and send it, with gun-case and shot, down to the station. Go up to Fort Brockhurst for luncheon; then skate on the lovely ice all round the moat. Give Miss Marryat a ride in a chair all round, and then let Riall have my skates, and go home and into Gosport to buy boots, leather pocket for note-book, &c. Walk home with the Isackes; and in the evening Edmeades comes to dine with us off a roast shoulder of mutton and a pheasant. Edmeades is off by 10.30; and then to bed.

Gosport to Southampton.
January 16, 1867.

Cab at door soon after 10. Good-bye; and leave word with Dr. Alder to go in and look after Mrs. Oliver. Off by 11.10 train. Excess of baggage. Take Cochrane (my gunner servant, since dead) to Bishopstoke, and there send him back. Straight to Thos. Hill, shipping agent, and leave with him all my baggage, except my bag, which I take to Radley's Hotel. Luncheon of excellent steak, and then by train to Sholing, where, hiring an execrable pair of skates, I kept my feet warm for an hour or so on the ice. Walked back. Dinner. Buy medicine-chest * &c. at chemist's. Get my hair cropped as short as possible.

---

* Ultimately this pocket medicine-chest, or rather box, proves most useful.

B

Southampton, R. M. S. P. Co.'s Steamship 'Tasmanian.'

January 17, 1867.

Up, and take a good bath and wash. Edmeades arrives by 9.18 train ; then we both breakfast on chops, and go to Hill's and the Royal Mail Steam Packet Co.'s offices. At 11.30 go off by the tender from the docks, and go on board the 'Tasmanian,' a fine long steamer lying off Netley. A little distance off is the ' Plata,' lately arrived, in quarantine, an ominous yellow flag at her fore, and, as it is said, sixty deaths have occurred during her home-ward passage from yellow fever. Luncheon, as usual, on board ship at noon. Very cold ; and Edmeades and I pace up and down the deck watching the other passengers and the shores of Southampton water. There are several Sisters of Charity on board, under Miss Sellon, bound for Honolulu. On the mails coming on board I recognize Inglis*, R.N., who was with me in the ' Gorgon;' he (as mail agent) and I sit next the Captain † at dinner. Edmeades leaves in the tug, and we also get under weigh about 3.20. Dinner at four, and after dinner we pass the Needles and leave the pilot. Funny W. Indian and officer of 16th Foot are very noisy with Californian Mrs. Scott and long-haired daughter. Lt.-Col. Mockler and wife ; Mil. Store Dept. Off. ; wife, sister of Dick Jones, R.A., and large family. P. L. S. initials ‡, followed by address ' Honolulu,' on quantities of luggage.

' Tasmanian,' at sea. N. lat. 48° 48', W. long. 6° 5'.

January 18, 1867.

Lovely fine morning, calm ; ship steady. 'Everybody in good spirits. Make acquaintance with various passengers. Table liberally supplied. A good number of passengers. My berth 189. A Danish doctor is my cabin com-panion, who I barely appreciate. Play at quoits with Funny man, and lose a bottle of beer. Distance from Terceira 1095 miles. The ' Tasmanian ' is 2445 tons register and 550 horse power.

' Tasmanian.' N. lat. 46° 17', W. long. 11° 27'.

January 19, 1867.

Barometer falls ·07 inch during middle watch. Nasty sea. Ship rolling. Few at breakfast. Bath under difficulties. Walk on deck in sou'-wester and oil-coat. Stowing jib and making snug. Everybody so-so. Funny man, very piano, and 16th Foot does not appear. Miss Sellon still confined to cabin. Miss Lysaght and another Sister of Mercy disappear at luncheon. Sleep for half an hour, and write up journal with Inglis's pen and ink. Get a nasty cropper on deck. Weather much warmer, about 60° Fahr. Distance from Terceira 831 miles. Barometer falls to 28·56. Pass centre of cyclone about midnight. Heavy cross seas.

' Tasmanian.' N. lat. 44° 20', W. long. 15° 47'.

January 20, 1867.

Still the only competitor for the order of the bath. Heavy sea. Speed decreasing. Barometer rises. Wind N.W. No divine service. Miss Ly-

---

* Staff-Comm. Frank Inglis, now Harbour Master at Portland.
† Capt. Leeds. ‡ P. L. S. = Priscilla Lydia Sellon.

saght appears on deck for a short time about luncheon time. Sun comes out. Still a good many gulls following in wake of vessel. No appearance yet of 16th Foot. Heavy seas at night. Wind rises. Shipping water all over. Distance from Terceira 633 miles.

'Tasmanian.' N. lat. 42° 42′, W. long. 19° 2′.

January 21, 1867.

Tall Barbadian tries effect of bath. Fine morning. Ship still rolling. Overcast, hazy, and finally rain. Chat with Miss Lysaght and Inglis. Write up journal after eight bells. Weather still chilly. 16th Foot still in cabin. Play chess with the Dane, and am beaten in two games. Distance from Terceira 435 miles.

'Tasmanian.' N. lat. 40° 41′, W. long. 22° 8′.

January 22, 1867.

Shipping heavy seas, with hard gale of wind right in our teeth. Clear day and warm sun. Mrs. Mockler and baby make their first appearance. May Scott recovered; sings " Home, sweet home," &c., after dinner; followed by Funny man, who sings " Pretty little Sarah " with effect. Distance from Terceira 263 miles.

'Tasmanian.' N. lat. 39° 3′, W. long. 25° 14′.

January 23, 1867.

Wind still in one's teeth. Not making much progress. Heavy cross seas. Taking in water. From Terceira distant 80 miles.

'Tasmanian.' N. lat. 37° 15′, W. long. 29° 0′.

January 24, 1867.

Just at 8 bells, attendant temporarily absent from sick bay, boat-swain jumps overboard in D. T. Disinclination to pick him up. Naval agent insists on life-buoys at least being picked up. Steamer rounds. Body picked up face downwards. Immediate appearance of white shark. Re-suscitation impossible. Body recommitted to deep directly. Floated, as stomach full of gas. From Sombrero 2132 miles. We had passed the Azores, which generally mark, at least in summer, the south-east trade-winds or at all events the limit of the variables ; but we experience severe south-west gales. To-day we were followed by a few kittiwakes (*Larus tridactylus*) and stormy petrels (*Thalassidroma pelagica*). The only vessels we had passed hitherto were small Portuguese brigantines trading between the Azores and Europe with fruit ; and we saw no more till we reached the West Indies.

" While south we go, blow high, blow low,
A thousand leagues away."

'Tasmanian.' N. lat. 35° 30′, W. long. 32° 14′.

January 25, 1867.

Gale of wind still blowing for the seventh day. If we had not been steam-

ing we should have it probably, like St. Paul, for fourteen days. The poor victim of yesterday has not appeased the spirits of Neptune and Æolus yet. From Sombrero 1948 miles. At night the phosphorescence of the sea was particularly brilliant, the surface scintillating with bright flashes from the small crustaceans, whilst large cylinders and globes of lambent light, proceeding probably from *Pyrosoma* and some of the Medusæ, glowed out and slowly disappeared in the wake of the vessel at the depth of a few feet.

"Gulf-weed passed from time to time, and patches of a species of *Fucus* (*nodosus*), or nearly allied form, evidently growing and participating in the wandering and pelagic habits of *Sargassum*. The floating islands of the gulf-weed of the Sargasso sea are usually from a couple of feet to two or three yards in diameter, sometimes much larger; we have seen on one or two occasions fields several acres in extent; and such expanses are probably more frequent nearer the centre of its area of distribution. They consist of a single layer of feathery bunches of the weed (*Sargassum bacciferum*), not matted, but floating nearly free of one another, only sufficiently entangled for the mass to keep together. Each tuft has a central brown thread-like branching stem studded with round air-vesicles on short stalks, most of those near the centre dead and coated with a *beautiful netted white polyzoon*. After a time vesicles so incrusted break off; and where there is much gulf-weed the sea is studded with these little separate white balls. A short way from the centre, towards the ends of the branches, the serrated willow-like leaves of the plant begin; at first brown and rigid, but becoming further on in the branch paler, more delicate, and more active in their vitality. The young fresh leaves and air-vesicles are usually ornamented with the stalked vases of a *Campanularia*. The general colour of the mass of weed is thus olive in all its shades; but the golden olive of the young and growing branches greatly predominates. This colour is, however, greatly broken up by the delicate branching of the weed, blotched with the vivid white of the incrusting polyzoon, and riddled by reflections from the bright blue water gleaming through the spaces in the network. The general effect of a number of such fields and patches of weed, in abrupt and yet most harmonious contrast with the lanes of intense indigo which separate them, is very pleasing." *Wyville Thomson*

' *Tasmanian.*'   N. lat. 34° 4', W. long. 34° 52'.

January 26, 1867.

Blowing harder than ever, a regular tornado. Ship pitching bows under and shaking all over. The seas a grand spectacle. The Captain says he has never before made the passage in the teeth of such a storm. Everybody longs for some rest and quiet, for the mere keeping on one's legs exerts one's muscles, and all complain of aching legs. Plenty of gulf-seaweed floating in patches. No water at all in baths. "Water, water! everywhere," &c. A cheap douche obtainable on the forecastle, but dangerous. Mrs. Scott has an epileptic fit again; and the want of her cheeriness adds a considerable gloom to our small society. The chief officer also unwell. As yet we have had but an unlucky voyage. I trust I am not a Jonah. Various surmises as to who is. Distance from Sombrero 1790 miles. The Doctor has an apoplectic fit; and the Danish doctor, Dr. Henius, comes out as a professional. General subsidence

'*Tasmanian.*' *N. lat.* 32° 35′, *W. long.* 37° 37′.

January 27, 1867.

Fine weather at last, but no water in the bath except hot water. No satisfaction to hear the bath-boy styled a fool. Make acquaintance with Lieut.-Col. Newdigate, late of the Coldstream Guards, an unobtrusive, quiet, gentlemanly fellow : he seems much interested in my projected travels. He is bound for Valparaiso, with an intelligent, delicate, deformed brother ; they are both very sea-sick still, and rarely make an appearance at meal-time. Rev. Parry performs service in the saloon after muster, and is very nervous and weak-voiced. Lovely sunny day. Most people on deck. Afternoon read ' The Land and the Book,' by Thomson, D.D. In the evening the children sing hymns. Fearful tale of yellow fever from our Irish R. C. passenger, who has had it, according to his own statement, twice. Starlight night. Sea not luminous. Distance from Sombrero 1626 miles. Miss Sellon is on deck for a few minutes in the afternoon ; she makes her appearance in conventual state, two sisters preceding her backwards with genuflexions, and a numerous staff follow bearing scent-bottles, books, and other paraphernalia. Her would-be regal manners are ridiculously out of place here.

'*Tasmanian.*' *N. lat.* 30° 12′, *W. long.* 41° 48′.

January 28, 1867.

Calm weather. Warm, muggy morning ; no sun. Water in bath scanty. Much improvement required. Barometer high, 30·28 ; thermometer 70°. Go forward after breakfast and get the third officer to cut off half a fathom of Hambro' line as a skipping-rope for little May : same little one is aged 13 years ; her step-sister Fanny 17$\frac{1}{2}$ years. From Sombrero 1371 miles.

'*Tasmanian.*' *N. lat.* 27° 44′, *W. long.* 46° 26′.

January 29, 1867.

Priscilla Lydia Sellon is daughter of Captain W. E. Sellon, R.N., and born about 1815, *i.e.* at present 52 years of age. The Bishop of Exeter having opened a public appeal on behalf of the spiritual destitution of Plymouth and Devonport, Miss Sellon went to reside there, opened poor-schools for boys and adults, and eventually established a house of Protestant Sisters of Mercy, thus becoming the founder of the conventual system in the Established Church. A great outcry was raised at first by a portion of the public against the institution at Devonport ; but Miss Sellon's cause was warmly espoused by the Bishop of Exeter, and ultimately triumphed over its assailants. Of late Miss Sellon has established sisterhoods of a similar kind at Bristol, in London, and elsewhere. From Sombrero 1086 miles.

'*Tasmanian.*' *N. lat.* 25° 24′, *W. long.* 51° 9′.

January 30, 1867.

Delightful weather. Amusing to watch the flying-fish, which dart with great velocity out of the water, without making, however, any regular fluttering movements with their fins, which they hold spread out with rapid vibration ; the pectoral fins do not act, as is generally supposed, like the wings of birds,

bats, and insects. Really the true cause of the movements of these fish (*Exocœtus volitans*) is the spring imparted to their body by means of excessively strong side muscles. They spring with greater velocity through the air because of less resistance, and their so-called wings act merely as a parachute. The peculiar formation of the mouth of the *Exocœtus* enables it to carry water during its flight in aid of respiration. From Sombrero 796 miles.

'*Tasmanian.*'　*N. lat.* 23° 0', *W. long.* 55° 37'.

January 31, 1867.

During a voyage through the tropics (to-day we have just crossed Capricorn), sunrise and sunset are ever subjects for contemplation : not only are the actual points of sunrise or sunset the scenes of glories unsurpassed in beauty and brilliancy of colour, but the exactly opposite points of the hemisphere are equally interesting, if more subdued and oftener more complicated in their succession of tints. Rays similar somewhat to those of the Aurora will be traced almost to the zenith, whence they contract to the E. & W. horizon: "*les rayons de crépuscule*" as the French call them, and "*Buddha's Rays*" by the Cinghalese. These must *not* be confounded with the "*sun drawing water*" and "*le bouillon qui chauffe,*" which phenomenon is caused by the rays of a higher sun through storm-clouds on the horizon. From Sombrero 512 miles.

'*Tasmanian.*'　*N. lat.* 20° 28', *W. long.* 60° 0'.

February 1, 1867.

Fine trade-wind abaft : spinning along at over twelve knots. Read Staunton. Play chess with Capt. Leeds, and am altogether overpowered. Pay Miss Lysaght five shillings for the little book-markers, for benefit of Miss Sellon's society. Sedlitz powder and colocynth pill. Commence letter to Clara after luncheon. From Sombrero 225 miles.

'*Tasmanian,*' *St. Thomas.*

February 2, 1867.

Pass Sombrero about 6 A.M. Small island, low, three miles circumference. Ships loading with sulphate of potash from beneath the guano : subject of dispute with Americans; pay English Government £700, and make £7000 out of it. Next Virgin Gorda, highest of the Virgin isles. Squalls. Write letter to Clara. Reach St. Thomas about 2 P.M., and do not enter further than quarantine station. About ship and round a point to anchorage in Little Krum Bay, separated from the real harbour only by an island and rocky ledge awash. Here we find the 'Danube,' 'Mersey,' and 'Eider' steamers, the 'Mersey' ready to start off. The 'Mersey' comes alongside and takes passengers and cargo for the Windward Islands, and the 'Danube' is to go on to Jamaica and take us in there. Afternoon and evening transhipping goods &c. to the 'Mersey.' Half the passengers leave us here for the islands, and we all go on board to inspect the steamer's accommodation &c., and in the evening take our grog on board the 'Mersey' and say goodbye to our friends. Send letter to Clara, which is to be posted and sent *viâ* Martinique. Major Newdigate, 60th Rifles, comes on board to join his

brothers ; at first, difficulty about admitting him on board as passenger, but Capt. Leeds is civil enough to allow him a passage.

Quarantine anchorage, ' Tasmanian,' St. Thomas.

February 3, 1867.

Leave our snug anchorage in Little Krum Bay before breakfast, preceded by the island steamer ' Mersey' on her way to Barbadoes, and by the ' Danube' steamer, which went on in advance to Kingston. The 'Tasmanian' steamer proceeds through the Gregory channel to the anchorage of the quarantine station outside St. Thomas's harbour. Here I take a sketch of the town and harbour. The coals are late in coming off, and doleful tales of the ravages from yellow fever and cholera are repeated. The flags are all hoisted half-mast in the town and shipping, and add to the gloomy forebodings and impressions. No church-service is held, as all hands are employed in transhipping cargo. Wolff, the Californian Jew, is very unwell, and is still more frightened than ill. Capt. Leeds criticises my sketch and adds a boat to it. French steamer, flying yellow flag, arrives, also an American steamer, by which we get news from New York and, through Atlantic Telegraph, later news from England. Coaling goes on all night, the niggers working for double pay on account of its being Sunday, and extra besides for working at night. Cameron, the agent here, seems an energetic man, but immunity from yellow jack is rather too favourable in his reports and letters on state of health, and in his statistics only shows the number of deaths occurring actually in St. Thomas, leaving to obscurity those deaths which were incurred before leaving here.

At sea, ' Tasmanian,' off Porto Rico Island.

February 4, 1867.

Finished coaling, and all quiet by 3 o'clock A.M.; steam up and under weigh half an hour later. Course W.S.W.; speed twelve knots. By 7 o'clock we pass Crab Island, and the whole day we are in sight of the fine high lands of Porto Rico Island, distant some half dozen miles. Tint with water-colour the sketch I had taken of St. Thomas. Play chess, and am beaten, after some good games, by the Danish Dr. Henius.

At sea, ' Tasmanian.'

February 5, 1867.

All day within sight of the south coasts of St. Domingo. We ought to go into Jacmel, but we only sight Alta Vela, and, by express desire of the mail agent, we go on to Jamaica, rather to the disgust of our only Jacmel passenger, viz. my friend Dr. Henius. A French transport, apparently bound for Mexico, under sail keeps pace with us for some time, and finally crosses our bows. When she alters her course we soon leave her behind, but we were going fast and doing over twelve knots. She turns out to be the ' Gironde,' and is wrecked the next day (Wednesday 6th) on one of the Kays south of Kingston.

At sea, ' Tasmanian,' Port Royal, Jamaica.

February 6, 1867.

Blue Mountains and Morant Point in view by noon. Dinner-hour changed

to 2 P.M. About 3 P.M. we pass the White Horses and arrive through the channel between the Kays off Port Royal, where the 'Danube' was in quarantine. We obtain pratique. Rooke and Sandes* come off and take me to Port Royal, the 'Tasmanian' steaming on to Kingston. Rooke and I do Port Royal and visit the Dygans. Rooke has comfortable quarters as governor of Fort Charles. Have a delightful wash before dinner. Rooke, Sandes, and two (3rd W. I.) officers compose the party.

Fort Charles, Port Royal, Jamaica.

February 7, 1867.

Feel the sun hot before the sea-breeze sets in. After breakfast Sandes, Rooke, and I go in the Fort boat to Kingston, have luncheon on board the 'Tasmanian,' and then walk out shopping with the Scotts. Invest in a puggery at three shillings, and some sugarplums for May. Return early to the Fort, walk to the Point, and in the evening after mess go to the Dygans with Jamieson the surgeon. See the women coaling the steamer. The 'San Francisco' steamer arrives from New York, bound for Greytown ; she obtains pratique, and passes on to Kingston. We watch her round the point from the battery outside Rooke's quarters. After I left Port Royal they had the yellow fever very bad, and Capt. Glascock was carried up to Up-park camp almost dying of it. He ultimately recovered, I believe.

Port Royal, Jamaica. 'Tasmanian.'

February 8, 1867.

Intellectual amusement of taking shots at a shaving-brush occupies us during a hot, lazy morning, in verandah. Glascock comes to join the garrison, after breakfast, in the market-boat. At 2 P.M. the 'Danube' steamer is released from quarantine, and steams alongside wharf at Kingston. At 2 P.M. Rooke and I leave Port Royal and have a good sail down to the Company's wharf at Kingston, meeting the 'San Francisco,' on board of which is Pim and staff for the Nicaraguan railway, bound for Greytown. Hail Pim and exchange a few words with him, and see Collinson, his chief engineer. We reach the 'Tasmanian' in time for dinner, and then go on shore with the Scotts for a drive : the traces break, so we walk back by moonlight, and look in to evening service at the church. Previous bad impressions of Kingston confirmed. Chaffing about the carpenter in evening. Sleep on board 'Tasmanian.' 'Tamar' arrives outside : exchange rockets and blue lights.

Kingston, Jamaica. 'Danube.' At sea. N. lat. 17° 51', W. long. 76° 50'.

February 9, 1867.

'Tamar' comes in from Colon. Slept on board the 'Tasmanian' for the last time ; woke early by donkey-engine transhipping cargo to 'Danube' steamer, Capt. Recks. Before breakfast passengers transhipped to the 'Danube.' Rooke stays to breakfast. About 10.30 we get under weigh, and wave our farewells to the 'Tasmanian,' proceed under steam to Port Royal, and leave there Rooke, who Sandes comes out in the boat to fetch. Not many new passengers ; one, an uncle and niece, very sea-sick and affectionate. Fresh trade blowing outside. Have distant view of the wreck of the 'Gironde,'

* Major W. Rooke, R.A., and Capt. H. T. T. Sandes, R.A., now Adjutant Yorkshire (West Riding) Artillery Volunteers.

French transport, and the 'Doris' frigate alongside it. Fanny and May rather sea-sick, also the Newdigates, with exception of the Major. Nice accommodation on board; pleasant saloon; No. 54 berth. Hot and stifling at night below; sleep in the saloon.

At sea. 'Danube.' N. lat. 14° 33', W. long. 78° 8'.
February 10, 1867.

Distance made 203 miles. Miss Lysaght is very ill, and her companions, viz. Miss Sellon and the Sisters of Charity, are most unkind in not believing how ill and weak she really is. It is the opinion of the Doctor and all of us that she should not proceed further under Miss Sellon's so-called care; and the Captain and Doctor both gently suggest her return to England. The hot and sultry weather, with the wind blowing with us, has a very relaxing effect, and we fear Miss Lysaght is in great danger of becoming so low that she may never rally. When this is mentioned to Miss Sellon or any of the nuns or maids (for they all act as waiting-maids for her), they laugh, and say it is all Miss Lysaght's fancy, and that she will soon get over it. All the officers and passengers, male and female, remark the selfishness of Miss Sellon as contrasted with the goodnature of Miss Lysaght; and in all our eyes the lay sister has much more claim to our respect than the Lady Superior, who has apparently grown too good for this earth, and looks upon all mortal men as sinful dust and ashes. I should like to have time and space to record a few of her many little meannesses. She is, out-and-out, the most selfish woman (sainted though she be) that I have ever met with.

'Danube.' At sea. N. lat. 11° 38', W. long. 79° 1'.
February 11, 1867.

Distance 190 miles; hot weather. My dear little daughter Katherine Rose born at 10.5 P.M. I do not hear of the above happy event until Wednesday 17th April. Miss Lysaght is still very ill; at last even the charitable Sisters of Mercy begin to believe that there is really something wrong with her health; but Miss Sellon will not dispense with even one of her party who minister to her wants. When painting on deck, she has one sister holding a palette, another mixing colours, a second holding paint-brushes, a third cleaning them, &c., and any one or all of them running up and down at her bidding for a cushion, or stool, or some luxury; meantime Miss Lysaght is at the mercy of a black stewardess. However, to-day, after strongest representations of Doctor and Captain, one of the Sisters is most ungraciously permitted to go and sit with poor Miss Lysaght. If Miss Lysaght dies, as is not at all improbable, I shall never cease to blame Miss Sellon for her heartless conduct; every one on board fully appreciates her mixture of ostentatious piety and utter selfishness.

'Danube.' Aspinwall.
February 12, 1867.

At 3 A.M. off Port Manzanilla; as it is not light, course is altered, and, accordingly, a sea washes into the port over where I am sleeping on the cushions in saloon, effectually awakening me up about five o'clock in time

to get my first view of the New World. The first piece of America which greets me is the mountain-range of the *Serro Llorana*, 3000 feet elevation, wooded to the summits. Have good view of coast about Porto Bello and woods, with overhanging mists; whilst by the time we have finished breakfast the steamer has rounded Punta Longarrenos and is well into Navy Bay.

Arrive at Aspinwall; some time in warping alongside the wharf. Go on shore and to Mr. Martin's office, where we consume B. and S. with Capt Rooks. Too late to catch the train, although in the evening the Newdigates succeed in getting across to Panama. I visit the manager of the Panama railway (Mr. W. Parker) and get a free pass across the isthmus and back. In the evening walk with the Scotts and Inglis round the point, by the church on the sea-shore. Aspinwall is a filthy town, of no pretensions whatever. The railway company is all potent here. Barely protected from the north by a slightly projecting coral reef, on which is a light and look-out, it is of made ground, on which stand warehouses, with five projecting piers of wood, stone, or iron screw-piles. Northern one, Railway Co.'s wharf; next, Liverpool Co.'s; then Royal Mail Steam, iron; Railway Coaling wharf and American Pacific Co.'s wharf. Iron foundry and workshops. Boston Ice Co. At Point is Mess-house, Railway Co., Martin's house, Hospital, sheds, fine warehouse, Martin's iron office, Harbour Master's, West India and Pacific Steam Co.'s Office. Billiard Rooms, Hôtel de France and Howard House the most reputable, behind filthy dens and slums; stagnant tidal pools and swamp behind. French Consul's house is building. Everybody looks fever-stricken, and may well do so, as the climate is deadly from the miasmatic vapours which are exhaled from the swamps and stagnant pools, but half filled in without drainage.

There is no railway-station, the trains starting from the street. The locomotives are of peculiar build and form, some having most absurd-looking balloon-like chimneys. The carriages are very long and hang on two pivots, each pivot on four wheels, and when in motion the body of the carriage swings and sways easily. The object of the two sets of four wheels is to enable the carriage to turn sharp corners. The engine fires are fed with wood, which heaped over the engine gives it a quaint appearance. A bell is kept constantly ringing on the locomotive as it passes along to warn the passers-by in the street. Every thing is of very rough and ready appearance, and there is very little attempt at show. In front of the engine is a projecting iron grating, "a cow lift," to clear away cattle or any thing from the line, which is nowhere enclosed as in England. There is only one class for all passengers; and the price of the journey of 47 miles is $25 or £5 across, and 2½*d.* for every lb. of luggage.

Aspinwall to Panama and back.

February 13, 1867.

Accompany Miss Lysaght to the railway cars. She begs me to attend on Miss Sellon, but I insist upon accompanying her; she is so weak that she is unable to walk all the distance without resting, although it is only a few yards, perhaps 150.

Mr. William Parker, superintendent of the Panama Railway, was subsequently shot in his office, in the presence of several other employés, on September 24th, 1868, by Mr. J. L. Baldwin, an engineer of the line, who then

shot himself. Parker died on the spot, and Baldwin was in a dying state. He was believed to have been suffering from delirium tremens when he committed the murder. At 7 A.M. we started for Old Morgan's Panama, the "town of gold," of the old filibusteros and pirates two centuries ago.

> "Then down we marched on old Panama,
> We the mighty buccaneers."

Morgan, the Welsh buccaneer, left Chagres with 1200 men on the 18th August, 1670; he reached Panama in ten days, which he at once attacked and sacked.

All the passengers for the Pacific side were in the train by 7 A.M. The last two cars only were for passengers. There was plenty of room, and the car nice and airy; you can walk from one car to another. The train was a long one, the other cars containing cargo freight, &c. The curves are very sharp, and looking from the after car you see the engine and foremost cars doubling round a corner as if it was impossible to follow where they led. I had a complimentary pass signed by Wm. Parker to Panama and back " at owner's risk of casualty " on it. Leaving the swamp we stopped a few miles on to lay in wood fuel for the engine, and here first saw turkey buzzards seated about perched on posts and dead trees watching for carrion. We were soon again on the track, never very fast, stopping every four miles at the track master's bungalow, very neat little houses with shrubs, orange-trees, limes, roses, &c. about them. The line ascends for the first 37 miles to 263 feet above the sea, and descends to the Pacific the remaining 10 miles. The forest scenery is charming, and reminded me of the woods in Madagascar—palms, palmistes, and the palmetto, bamboos, and wild plantains. One tree covered with yellow blossoms, a mass of golden flowers, was very conspicuous. Deep coloured creepers of magenta hues like the *Ipomœa* clustered here and there. Lovely creeping ferns of every imaginable delicate shape garlanded the palms and larger timber trees. Orchids in large bunches especially selected the decayed branches of dying trees, and it was tantalizing to obtain only a passing glance of some extra gorgeous orchid. Acres of a large species of *Osmunda* were passed, and I picked up the silver fern growing under the very rails of the permanent way. Butterflies of brilliant hues there were plenty of, but the birds were not very numerous to view.

We arrived at Panama at 11 o'clock after 4 hours, and proceeded to the Aspinwall Hotel there. Panama is a regular Spanish town, and similar to any old Spanish town of the south of Europe. Remains of fortifications, cathedral, Jesuit colleges, and churches, ruinous buildings, &c. Tiled roofs, verandahs, and jalousies are predominant. It was very hot in the streets. From the southern extremity of the town seawards there is an enchanting view of wooded promontories and islands. There were a pretty marmozet and two pretty monkeys that I saw, besides several jaguar-skins, in the shops. Returning to the hotel I breakfasted, and at 1.45 P.M. walked with Col. Newdigate to the railway-station, where I again mounted the passenger car; and as it was a special train, we spun along and did the whole passage back, only twice stopping, in two hours, so that I got back to the ship in time for the 5 o'clock dinner. I was never less fatigued with a ninety-five miles railway journey, and altogether my health is much better than when I left England; I really think that heat agrees with my constitution.

Aspinwall. '*Danube*,' *at sea. N. lat.* 9° 40', *W. long.* 8° 20'.

February 14, 1867.

Distance 30 miles. Up early. Send a note, by way of valentine, to little May Scott by Mr. Martin, who is going over to Panama. By breakfast-time we got under weigh, and, with a nice breeze from N.E., feel the atmosphere cooler and more healthy. The vessel seems much quieter and empty now of all the passengers except Dr. and Mrs. Grand or Grant, a French-American adventurer and his wife, and a Caraccas Spanish Colonel, Del Olio, who is always boasting of his warlike achievements, wounds, and bravery till I begin to suspect he is a coward. Sea-sickness makes him roar aloud, so that he disturbs us at dinner, and the Captain kindly sends him some curry, the sight of which brings on a relapse. There is always plenty of yellow fever at Aspinwall and Panama. People at former place buried by rail out of the town.

*At sea. '*Danube*,' off Greytown.*

February 15, 1867.

After eight bells steered in towards land, which was very hazy and difficult to make out. Latitude was out, so made the coast, not far from Monkey Point, and had to put back, coasting, so that it was some time before we distinguished the few houses and low-lying town of San Juan del Norte, or Greytown. We had to anchor about 3.40 P.M. at least a mile outside the bar, which was bad, a heavy surf breaking, we rolling considerably. A mail agent came off in canoe, bringing me a note from Capt. Pim, telling me to land at once, if possible, with my traps. The man in charge of canoe refused to take me; and consequently I stopped on board, and had, at all events, a much more comfortable dinner and bed on board than I should have had on shore. As I was about to quit comforts for some months, I was not sorry to have one more night's comfort. In consequence of recurrence of fatal accidents, the boats of the R. M. S. P. Co. are strictly forbidden to leave the ship on any pretence, however calm ; so that passengers are wholly dependent on the canoes and lighters from the shores. Greytown not unlike City of Eden in '*Martin Chuzzlewit.*' Also river San Juan and steamers.

*Greytown. River San Juan. The '*City of Rivas*' steamer.*

February 16, 1867.

Up by daylight, and, after bath, to breakfast. The Vice-Consul Paton came off in a canoe; on the Captain's asking him, he took me ashore. Landing about 8 A.M. I found Pim at Hollenbeck's, and learnt we were to start that afternoon up the river. Breakfasted with party consisting of Collinson and Deering, the engineers, Col.* and Mrs. Richard Maury (former son of Commodore Maury, U.S.N., of geographical fame), nice little wife and child. They are going out to Chontales district to take charge of the Javali mine, belonging to Central American Association. Permit obtained for passing traps. Canoe bought and christened '*Sue.*' Weather charming. Diggers here from Chontales Co. Mine going to England with gold. Dine with above party and a Col. Del Olio at Mrs. Deziman's, where they are stopping ; Pim at Hollenbeck's. Embark on board the '*City of Rivas*' steamboat, drawing 18 inches water, stern paddle-wheel. On the

* Col. Richard Maury.

river San Juan the Transit Company have several of these river-boats plying. Formerly they could steam right up the river, but at present they only ply between the rapids, causing frequent transhipments and consequent expense. It has been proposed to make artificial shoots to evade them, something like the Canadian portages. These river steamers are built expressly for the purpose of traversing shallow waters. Their bottom is quite flat and divided into compartments, the first deck being only about eighteen inches above the water, from which it is divided by no gunwale. On this deck is the driving-machinery—the vertical boiler and furnace in the bow and the horizontal engines in the stern, over which projects a huge paddle-wheel whose floats only dip the water for the depth of a foot. Above this deck is a platform on which are the passengers, with wooden pillars supporting a superstructure or hurricane-deck. The appearance of these huge, snorting, floating houses with their tall steeple-engines, and vomiting clouds of smoke with sparks from the wood fuel, has a peculiar effect as contrasted with the primæval scenery through which the river winds its tortuous way. Get under weigh about 6 P.M. and proceed, with bright moonlight, up river San Juan, steaming all night, now shoving off with polancas, now backing off sand-bank, now running alongside to load with wood fuel. Haunts of alligators scented of musk; weird wood and forest scenery on either side. Sling hammocks where we can. Caribs and cook engaged to accompany expedition. Mosquito Indian Abraham, his romantic attachment to Mrs. Maury. Chat with Southern Colonel. Brandy I brought acceptable to whole party. Badly provisioned. Pigging it. Begin to realize what I am on.

The ‘City of Rivas’ steamer. River San Juan. The ‘Managua’ steamer.

February 17, 1867.

Velocity of current 1 mile to 1½ mile per hour. This morning had not the slightest idea that it was Sunday. Awoke at daylight and find that our raft-like steamer is moored to a tree, simple and effective. Bathe by means of a bucket. Alligators preclude idea of swim. Under weigh, or rather let go of the bushes, but soon stuck fast on a bank, and we have to transfer cargo and passengers to lighten the boat as far as the junction of the Colorado. The ladies are put into canoe (viz. Dr. and Mrs. Grand, Col. and Mrs. Maury), as it goes faster; we, viz. Pim, Collinson, Griffiths, Fairbairn, Deering, and self in lighter, under sail with dingy. Col. Del Olio steers. Very hot sun. Magnificent trees, creepers, suspended birds’ nests, islands, snags, &c., few clearings; visit one of Eugene Costa’s in which are planted plantains, limes, cocoa, and coffee. Traces of alligators. Arrive at the Colorado river and at once go on board the ‘Managua’ river steam-boat, commanded by Capt. Parker; his wife on board. He has been up river Frio. Lovely moonlight. Dinner off salt meat, warree, and ham. The flesh of the *warree* any thing but so tender and savory as Samuel A. Bard would have us believe. Comforting assurance, that if you do this or that you will be sure and get the fever; in fact, that whatever you do you will be sure and get it. Fever-stricken look of the few settlers along some of the clearings. Low marshy banks, &c. See Mark Tapley’s ‘Voyage up the Eden’; might be the identical river, as far as description goes.

Junction of Colorado River and San Juan River. The ‘Managua’ steamer.

February 18, 1867.

After a wash, by means of a bucket (emptying several over me over the side), set to work fishing and, after a short time, hook a savallo of about

2½ pounds. Col. Maury catches another. Breakfast off more salt wild hog and salt salmon; savallo doubtful! Get my first shot at an alligator across the stream, 300 yards. Make up cartridges. Go up the river with Collinson and Col. Maury in canoe. Shoot a kingfisher and a heron get. Capital close shot at two alligators, which splash into the river, and no mistake, when they feel the Enfield bullets. Lovely tree ferns on bank. Green small iguana. Paddle back to dinner; more salt provisions; scouse or soaked biscuit, tomatoes, and good Californian potatoes. Towards evening the flats come up slowly with rest of cargo, and, the ' Cora' remaining, we get up steam and go off after dinner. It is a lovely evening, glowing sunset. Col. Maury has a couple of shots from my rifle at the alligators, which seem pretty plentiful about here. Dr. and Mrs. Grand amuse themselves with pistol practice on the hurricane-deck. On board 'Managua' were sort of shelves put up for sleeping accommodation, in three sets of tiers. Although I carefully arranged my mosquito-bar (Yankee term), still all through the night my as yet unaccustomed flesh was made a meal of by divers insects. Above the Colorado river (which is the main river) the river is broader, more rapid, and deeper; in fact it is actually navigable. Pensile nests of oriole covering cotton-trees [*]. Crested oriole, or *Cacicus cristatus*, size of a jackdaw.

The ' Managua' steamer. River San Juan. The ' Cora' steamer. Machuca Rapids. Castillo Viejo.

February 19, 1867.

Machuca. Halt about 4 A.M. below the rapids. Heavy mists hanging about the trees, and every thing dripping wet. Plenty of fish. Lose my line and hook. Canoe alongside with alligators' eggs. Transhipped to 'Cora' steamer, a smaller one, above the rapids, the baggage going in canoes, and most of us walking round the point, where a path is cleared for the purpose. Scarlet small frogs. Little girl on board very ill. Islands formed in river by wrecks of steamers. Remains of one blown up with filibusters. Reach Castillo Viejo and sketch. No. 2 dinner on shore; fish from shore. Walk up to Nelson's Hill by the Fort. Strong rapids at bend of river. 'Cora' steamer goes back to Machuca to fetch up remaining cargo. We sling our hammocks at rather close quarters in a hut, called by its proprietor an hotel. ' Cora' arrives after dark, and ' City of Leon' steamer arrives before morning. Macaws flying at great height in pairs; their screaming noise and ugly heads. Various water-fowl, herons, &c., egrets. Shallow water; twisting river; short reaches. Thick woods. Hot sun. The little girl's attack of illness has strong symptoms of cholera. Very bad, and almost dead during night; but, by application of strong remedies, she recovers. At the very ends of boughs, where the twigs cannot sustain the weight of a monkey, pensile nests, nearly a yard long, of the crested cassique, on the highest trees.

The ' City of Leon.' River San Juan. The ' Tipitapa' steamer. San Carlos. River Frio.

February 20, 1867.

Hammock uncomfortably slung. No mosquitoes, luckily, as our curtains could not be put up. Early breakfast, and go on board the 'City of Leon' steamer, lying above the rapids. Goods transferred on trucks along a tramway. Got off at 7 A.M. River Savallo about 10 o'clock. The Toro rapids.

---

[*] " *Bombax ceiba.*"

Shoot an alligator at 20 yards. Less wood and palms; bamboo. After breakfast on board, go in boat up the river Savallo a few yards, and, with Pim in front, cut a path with machetes to some hot springs that come bubbling up, steaming hot, forming a small marsh. Proceed under steam. Shores now flatter and marshy. About dinner-time we sight Fort San Carlos, and steam into the lake round the wreck of a steamer, and lay alongside the 'Tipitapa' steamer, a lake-going, paddle-wheel steamer. After dinner Pim, Deering, Col. and Mrs. Maury in canoe, I and two Caribs in a dingy, pull to the fort and then across the San Juan and up the Frio river *, of unenviable notoriety, for a few hundred yards; take a few angles, and, as it gets dark, return. See plenty of iguanas on the trees bordering the placid stream. Return by dark on board the 'Tipitapa,' and, getting under weigh, steer for San Miguelito, about twenty miles distant to the N.W. About 10.30 or 11 P.M. we make out the dim outline, through fog, of San Miguelito and anchor, after sending boat ashore to ascertain that this is the place, for a few huts, invisible in the dark, is all that forms the village of San Miguel. We anchor about a mile off the shore, and, in spite of many discomforts, sleep well.

Lake of Nicaragua. Steamer 'Tipitapa.' San Miguelito.

February 21, 1867.

Up early. Deering, Collinson, Pim, &c. off early, mounted, to prospect. I wait and breakfast on board, then take Dr. Grand and Mrs. Grand, Mrs. Maury and child on shore. Capt. Fish and myself then go off towards Bernado Island in a boat, so as to take soundings, and find the average depth to be 13 feet right across mouth of bay. Lovely view of volcanos Madora and Ometepec to the S.W. Sea gets up, and we have a hard pull back to steamer. In afternoon go on shore, find the ladies of the party at Montenegro's house, where they dine. I take a walk through the woods, and make my first acquaintance with the Garrapata tribe. Pim comes back to supper, having fixed a good start, and Collinson comes to say good-bye &c. Deering remains on shore. Griffiths and stores located in a house hired on the hill. Start off, steaming by moonlight, and in less than a quarter of an hour we strike on the Anna Maria rock, to the great dismay and confusion of all. Various characters of those on board shown up. The loudest swaggerers (notably our fire-eaters Del Olio and Dr. Grand) are most in a funk. Water comes in fast; a very bad hole. (Fate of Dr. Grand see Monday, 9th of April.) Start off canoe to Castillo Viego with Capt. Fish, for the 'City of Leon' steamer to come up to our assistance. Land the ladies and their husbands, Spaniards, &c. Occupied all night in stopping the leak and pumping. It is to be feared that it is a regular case of come to grief.

---

* The *Rio Frio* comes down from the interior of Costa Rica, and its inaccessible banks of impenetrable jungle are inhabited by tribes of Indians of whom little is known. They are called *Guatusos*, and are said to have fair or at least red hair and to be generally lighter than the usual Central-American Indians. Indeed some go so far as to trace their origin to the buccaneers. Anyhow they are fierce and intractable, and many expeditions have returned with some of their party wounded by arrows from their unseen foes. The Guatusos are also said to inhabit trees, on which they form platforms, during the inundations to which their lowland country is subject. They use stone implements, bone hooks, &c.

Anna Maria Rock. Bay of San Miguelito. Lake Nicaragua.

February 22, 1867.

Lie down about 1 A.M. in a bed prepared for Mrs. Grand, and sleep comfortably till broad daylight. Take bearings. Pumps keep the water through leak tolerably under. Fairbairn and Collinson come off in a canoe, and fetch some things. Sketch the bay. Captain Pim goes on shore after breakfast, and I go in a little boat and take soundings round the vessel ; find the reef extends about two ships' lengths on port bow, line of San Miguel Island. Comes on to blow, and squally. Land all our luggage and stores. Go on shore in the afternoon, and take up quarters in the house hired by Collinson. There is a slight partition, behind which Mrs. Maury establishes herself, and we swing our hammocks in rather close quarters, and some sleep on the ground. The ' City of Leon' steamer arrives about midnight. Mosquitoes rather annoying. Bongo hired ; and, as it is very leaky, have it patched up. The Spanish Colonel and Dr. Grand try to outbid Captain Pim, and have great quarrelling among themselves. Mr. Deering already at work with his level. The cholera has more than decimated San Miguelito, so that there are several houses empty. All the doors have prayers fastened on them to keep the cholera out.

San Miguelito. Nicaragua Lake. Nanzital Island. Canoe.

February 23, 1867.

Loading the bongo and canoe both nearly to water's edge. Colonel Maury and Mrs. sail with Fairbairn in the bongo about 11 A.M., with fair wind, for San Ubaldo. Captain Pim and self about noon, in the canoe, communicate with the ' Leon,' and have the happiness to see the steamer ' Tipitapa' got off the rock, and both steamers steam away* for San Carlos. Wind on the quarter, we rip along at five miles an hour ; gunwale almost under, but our heavy load renders the canoe stiff. Crew, Thomas and Julio. Much burnt by sun, although rather cloudy. Fine clear evening, with brilliant sunset effects. Behind Island of Madera and Ometepec two volcanic cones. Island of Zapatero is also visible in the evening. The bongo's sail is just visible in front of us all the way, and we slightly gain on them. At night we make fast to an island, one of the Nanzital group, light a fire, and have dinner on shore. Captain Pim and self then sleep in the pirogue, and Thomas and Julio on shore. Various queer noises of birds and insects. All kinds of water-fowl and duck abound on the shores of the lake. Few, if any, Kingfishers. America the poorest part of the world for Kingfishers. No signs of sharks or alligators. There is no doubt but that sharks do exist in the lake, and traverse the San Juan from the lake to the ocean. Similarly the alligator (?) is found in fresh and salt waters.

Lake Nicaragua. San Ubaldo.

February 24, 1867.

Moon rises, and at 3 A.M., by its light, we leave our bivouac on the Nanzital and hoist sail. I sleep most of the way, until we arrive at San Ubaldo, about 8 A.M., where the Maurys have previously arrived at midnight. I get

* Before leaving the bay the unfortunate 'Tipitapa' again got on shore near the San Miguel island, but again came off, scathed, and steamed to San Carlos, where she was soon put in trim for the Lake passage.

a bathe: and we all breakfast under a large stone shed, substantially built, with a tiled roof. In the little bay lie scattered pieces of machinery awaiting transport to the mines, distant some thirty miles. Captain Paul, the Captain of the San Domingo mine, is fortunately here, and is able to escort Mrs. Maury, with her husband, up to Javali. Poor little Mrs. Maury is plucky enough, and was present at many battles in the south. She is a regular southerner, and very outspoken with her sentiments. Her courage, however, utterly failed her on her journey up to the mines, and she was utterly broken down before reaching Javali; and indeed well she might be, for a more heartbreaking road I never met with in all my life. After the Maurys leave we reembark in the good canoe ' Sue,' now furnished with a larger sail; in fact about as much as she can carry. Off we go, considerably lightened, no chairs or sherry, more sea-room, and a fresher breeze, before which we scud, taking in water; all over wet through and baling. By sunset wind goes down, and we stop at an island called Polena, just beyond the islets Muertos. Good view of Mombacho, the volcano near Granada.

Isles Muertos, Polena or Polona, on the Lake to Tipitapa. Estero Panaloya.

February 25, 1867.

Under weigh at 4 a.m., by light of the moon. Bitten by insects, and not much refreshed. Fine breeze. Try entrance of Malacatoya river; try back, and take southern entrance to Los Cocos. Lagoon formed by sand bar. Scare an alligator, pass the village of Los Cocos, and up the river to ferry-house on north side of river, highroad between Granada and Chontales. Breakfast at Ferry. Paso Real, the Royal Ferry. Good Tiste (chocolate, maize, and water). Snooze in hammock. Off again in canoe, up the river Tipitapa. Alligators: first monkeys. Forest scenery similar to San Juan river; less traffic. Derbyshire's hacienda and clearing hall at a hacienda below the falls. Hire a carreta, with four bullocks, to transport the canoe and baggage beyond the falls. Brazil-wood cut down for sale. Plenty of horses, cattle, few sheep. Children hunting iguanas. Dine off tough fowl, and two bottles of Fairbairn's invaluable beer, of which not much remains. Walk through woods in the evening. Shoot an iguana and a black monkey (*Cebus albifrons*) with white face and neck (a handsome animal); give both to the guide, as my apparatus for preserving has never turned up. Wound a quail, which escapes. Come to remains of an old bridge built by Spaniards below the falls; wooden upper works repaired by Nicaraguans. Good view of the falls. Curious sulphur-springs close to the bridge, on the right bank of river. Halt for the night at Tipitapa village. Sleep on ox-hide bed. Admiration of natives at looking down the bright barrels of the breach-loading gun. Universal search of inmates for jiggers and garrapatas (candle in hand) before turning in.

From Tipitapa Village, Lake Managua, to Managua.

February 26, 1867.

Up at daylight, and bathe in the Falls of Tipitata. Afterwards examine sulphur-springs, which bubble up on the right bank of the river close to the bridge, and incrusts the rocks, sticks, and leaves with sulphur; the water boiling hot, flowing into the river. Sketch the Falls from the bridge, about 50 yards below the Falls, which are about 12 feet high. Droves of cattle driven in across the bridge. Picturesque costume of Vaqueros. Humming-

c

birds for the first time, very tame. Tame brown monkey with black face, ugly one. Talking parrot, imitating cries of Vaqueros. Fowls pecking at a dead armadillo brought in by the herdsmen. Mules with packs, not girths. Embark after breakfast, and run against rocks; intricate passage *. Black lava-field and dark iguanas, called chuli, on opening the lake of Managua. See the volcano of Leon in front, and Momotombo to the right of it. Carry away boom. Squalls. Running before the wind. High seas. Ship green water. Baling out and only just in time to reach Managua, swamped in the heavy surf, and wet through in shirt and breeches. General dread of cholera, and dull appearance of Managua, Plaza Cathedral, Barracks, adobe houses, our dwelling apartment, cockpit dinner, &c. Procession to avert cholera. Churches filled with Indian worshippers and black priests. Pim goes to see Martinez the President. Neighbouring room supposed case of cholera. Make up prescription 'for a woman who has had nothing to eat for six days. Tolling of bells. Thomas goes through vocabulary of Mosquito country. Howling winds. Send linen to the Lavanderos. Sneezing fit. Congress not sitting.

At Managua.

February 27, 1867.

Awoke by any amount of cocks crowing—the fighting cocks being tied by the leg around the cockpit and round the compound; one old fellow in the centre. Bathe in a fine solid wooden washtub. Watch some tiny hummingbirds opposite. Slight diarrhœa, so take a lead and opium pill. In doors nearly all day till about 2 P.M., when I walk with Captain Pim through the town, past the market and slaughterhouse above the town. Cactus-hedges. Out of the town by narrow road through uncultivated country; steep banks on either side. Various lizards. Up a hill, when we suddenly come on the deep lake of Tiscapa, evidently the extinct crater of a volcano, nearly circular, with precipitous sides, densely wooded. Women naked to waist washing. Drove of mules watering and cattle. Sketch. Notice red-crested woodpecker (*Celeus castaneus*). Captain Pim unable to finish his business with the officials, so have to stop over to-morrow. Linen back from wash; no attempt at ironing. Another procession in the evening. Buy pair of slippers, and have my boot-toe mended for 2 dollars. Thomas and Domingo engaged in making a jib for canoe, and carpenter makes a rudder. New polanca provided for sprit.

At Managua.

February 28, 1867.

Ten cases of cholera reported by Don Antonio during the past night. Visited by the Priest Rafael Ramierez before breakfast, show him breech-loader, &c. Pack up after breakfast. Boys employed making alforeas and arranging tackle. See rudder fitted to boat. Don Antonio da Silva goes away to Masaya to meet the new President. Visit General Martinez at the Government-house. This is his last day of being President of the Republic. The General shows us a magnificent eagle from the mountains of Segovia, which form a magnificent panoramic background to the lake of Managua as seen from the town. In the evening pack up a few things in our *alforeas* or saddle-bags, and put the bulk of our baggage away in the care of Señor

---

* Proposed canal almost impracticable.

Prospero, the hotel-keeper.   Eagle above mentioned is the crested harpy (*Thrasaëtus harpyia*), or courageous eagle.

Managua to Pueblo Nuevo.

March 1, 1867.

Off at 2 A.M., by starlight, across the lake in the canoe, as far as Chiltepec promontory. The waters of the lake were calm and smooth, although rolling undulations were sufficient to make the boat unsteady. By daylight it came on to blow ; the white curling crests soon appeared, and we run as soon as possible, very wet and baling, under the lee of the point. Here we put away for Mohabita, but a squall carries away mast and sail &c., and we have to paddle hard to shore under a jury rig of the jib hoisted on a polanca. A slight bay gives us shelter to land near Nagarote ; and here we light a fire, cook breakfast, and dry our clothes. I shoot a fine bittern, a squirrel, and a chuli or striped iguana. Sketch the active volcano of Momotombo from here. See a whole colony of white-faced monkeys. Of course get covered with garrapatas, which cover the bushes. About 12.15 set sail again, the wind having moderated ; and after a run of ten miles in about two hours, land in a heavy surf on the beach at Mohabita. Here we leave the boat with the pilot, and walk (Thomas and Julio carrying our traps, the mules not having arrived) through wooded country over a limestone ridge, on which is a deep well surrounded with tall cactus-hedge, where we hot and thirsty mortals are glad to drink ; and, after about six miles, we reach Pueblo Nuevo. Put up in a comfortable home built of adobe or sun-dried mud bricks. The streets are all at right angles, with tall pillar-like rows of cactus for fences. Two mules and a horse arrive for us before dark. The Plaza is enclosed for a bull-fight to-morrow, for which we cannot wait.

Pueblo Nuevo to Leon.

March 2, 1867.

Father and mother's birthday.   There is a manufactory of pottery and earthenware jars at Pueblo Nuevo. Usual breakfast on tortillas*, eggs, and frijólas†. Mount our mules and ride on the highroad to Leon, across a rising plain thinly wooded. Plenty of chulis, very tame, lizards. Plenty of well-conditioned cattle feeding, but no signs of cultivation beyond an occasional plantain patch or a *petraro* with maize, now ready to be gathered. After three leagues we halted, and eat a few oranges. Several parties met us on their way to the bull-fight at Pueblo Nuevo ; and we ride on through the same sort of country for four more leagues, when we arrive through a more open space of country from which we can see around for miles, from El Viejo to the north-west the range of volcanoes to Momotombo on the east. Halt at a hut at a spot called El Convento ; ask for *tiste*, but none to be had, so have to be content with water. The woman presents us with a fruit of delicate taste. Another league across an elevated plain, mostly cleared, and with a magnificent panoramic view of the country all round. Sight the cathedral of Leon, and soon after enter that town. Paved streets, gutter in centre ; no foot pavement. Plenty of churches. Ride through the Plaza, and down the Calle Nacionale to the café ' *Leon del Oro*,' kept by an Italian sailor. Morris is ill with fever at Mrs. Cauty's house. Quantities of small pigeons and doves, viz. *Cola larga, tortola,* and *carmelita.* Hedges of columnar cactus or " organo."

* Tortillas are cakes = dampers made of maize.   † Frijólas = beans and other pulse.

Leon.

March 3, 1867.

Visit Mr. Morris, who is prostrated with fever, brought on whilst surveying the line from Castañon Bluff, the south-west extremity of Realejo Harbour. He and Sonnernsten have cut a piquet of 18 miles 900 yards, and chained it, but not levelled it, in twenty-four days. Go to see one of the churches, and also the American Minister Mr. Dickenson, wife, and married daughter; the latter very agreeable and pleasant, lately from the States, having come by the San Francisco steamer. After dinner go up the outside roof of the cathedral, and have a sketch (very hasty one) of the chain of volcanoes from thence. Very hot all day. Cockfighting greatly in vogue; dozens of people traversing the streets each with a cock under his arm. Apparently much hotter than near the lakes; no refreshing breeze. Uncomfortable little old stable by way of a room, without ventilation. Max Sonnernsten, an ex-Prussian corporal, arrives from the cutting, with the two Caribs, Simon and Perry. Procession round the town, with music &c., escorting the Saints, and invoking their protection from *La Peste*, the cholera, which is so much dreaded.

Leon to Castañon Bluff.

March 4, 1867.

Up at 4.30 A.M. After a hasty cup of coffee, leave by 5, mounted—Sonnernsten, on large grey flea-bitten Rosinante, and a very Don Quixote himself in appearance, leads; Captain Pim, on a pretty long-tailed little horse, following; self on large grey mule, Perry on another, and our mozo carrying a *maleta*. After leaving the town, we pass through the suburban village of Subtiaba, with its ancient church and ruins of conventual buildings, the first built by the Spaniards on exploring the country. Enter the woods just as the sun is rising behind Momotombo's conical peak, a long narrow *carreta* track. Pass Rancho of San Cristoval; rather impracticable levels here. Plenty of parroquets chattering. At 8.30 come to salt-lagoon near Pacific coast. Salt-works, evaporation in earthenware pots. Poor breakfast. Mangrove bushes and sand bar. Watering-place of Los Salinas. Remains of boothies and shanties of straw and palm-branches, which are used as bathing-houses during the season just over. Bad water. Marshes. Eleven miles of hot burning sand. Great difference in tides. Distant rocks and breakers. Remains of turtles. Reach harbour of Realejo. Opposite we see Corintho, and vessels at anchor. Ride back by sunset. Get caught in dark. No moon. Splendid phosphoric breakers of the Pacific rollers. Return and sleep at the salt-works. Captain Pim gives me up his hammock, as I am rather knocked up by the sun and bad water. Rude natives on the roof above where I sleep.

Los Salinas to Leon.

March 5, 1867.

Up at daybreak, and, mounting our poor tired steeds, who had been hard up for water all day since yesterday, ride back. At the first stream of fresh water our steeds are eager to drink, and felt much refreshed. Get a sketch of Subtiaba on my way back. Breakfast at the 'Leon del Oro.' Visit cotton-ginning machine of Deshon's, and go to see Mr. Morris, who is evidently much better, but not fit yet to be moved. Try to get to the top of the

cathedral, but cannot find the man who has the key, and so enter inside, where I witness a grand procession round the interior, and evening vespers. No music, as I had hoped to hear.

Leon.

March 6, 1867.

Some men bring in a squirrel for sale in a revolving cage. Great ringing of bells, and women returning from early mass at the different churches, marked on their foreheads with a black cross. Purchase tortoise-shell, spurs, sandals, &c. Go to the store of Madura & Co., and purchase Guatemala cloth for clothes, &c. In the afternoon accompany Captain Pim to the Government-house and office of the Prefect of Leon; deliver letter to Don Clito Majorga, asking for a certificate relative to railway construction between Los Salinas and Leon. In the evening a refusal to the request arrives. I get a sketch of the old Spanish bridge across the brook, a picturesque old ruin. Take wine in Derbyshire's room.

Leon to Momotombo.

March 7, 1867.

Up before daylight, and Captain Pim and self, accompanied by Max Sonnernsten and the mozo, ride past El Convento by a different route to a hacienda near lake Tigre. See some wild boars and a deer, but do not get a shot. Captain Pim kills a ('*pava*' or '*guan*') penelope, a species of wild turkey, which we consume at the hacienda, under volcano of Axuseo. Ride on to *ancient* locale of the ruins of old Leon, close to the lake, and there, leaving Sonnernsten, embark in canoe with pilot, Julio, Perry, Simon, Thomas, and ourselves. There is a nasty wash on, as there always seems to be on this lake; and we get close *under* Momotombo, and land to have supper close by the hot springs that issue from its base. Reembark, and have a stormy wet passage round the point of the promontory on which the volcano Momotombo stands. Here the pilot says he knows a sheltered cove, so we stand in; and on reaching shallow water are instantly filled with the waves. We drag up the canoe, and manage to sleep a little with what dry things there are; and the waterproof sheet proved invaluable, as it had, indeed, the whole way.

Momotombo viâ Momotombitra to Matiares.

March 8, 1867.

First thing, some time after the sun is up, take my gun and go into the woods to see what I can. Bring back a wild turkey. See a deer, lots of reddish-brown monkeys, a young alligator, and a large one. Shot a macaw. The wind still blowing fresh, we wait till after noon, when, it lulling for a time, treacherously, we are tempted to launch our frail craft and trust ourselves again on the waters. Of course, as soon as we are well off the shore it blows harder than ever, and we were all on the weather gunwale washed through and through, and the lee gunwale under water. Just before reaching the island of Momotombitra a white squall causes us to take in all sail and lie down in the bottom of the canoe until the 'temporale' is over. Then we paddle up to the island, which seems guarded watchfully by stormy squalls and huge alligators; these latter were swimming about, with their huge mouths open, in dozens. We land and examine a few insignificant, yet

interesting remains of the Indian idols on the shore, and then paddle close in shore round the lee side of the island. As we rounded each projecting point *herds* of large alligators, disturbed in the next bay, would hurry down into the waters; the whole shore was literally alive with them, and the lake waters as well. It was quite nervous to meet a heavy curling roller round the weather point of the island with a gigantic alligator swimming along on the top of it, with his fierce teeth and malignant eyes glaring on you. I was not sorry when, after crossing as near the wind as we could, we reached the calmer waters, six miles north of Matiares, to which place we paddled, and landed, very wet; glad of fire and supper on the sand. Go up into village, and have difficulty about mules. Meet Frank Mortara, a courier, who has letters for Captain Pim. Usual cholera procession.

Matiares to Managua.
March 9, 1867.

Los Bestias, on being taken to water, and having already been paid for (four and half dollars each), made their escape, and caused at least a couple of hours' delay before they could again be brought to the scratch. Matiares has a bad reputation for its inhabitants; and we certainly suffered severely from the fleas *et hoc genus omne*. Chocolate and milk, with turtles' eggs and tortillas, prepared us; and we were soon on our way through the woods, for nowhere do there appear any cultivated clearings. The carreta track would not be bad if it were not that wherever a fallen tree had obstructed the road a detour is formed to right or left, and the obstruction not removed. Leaving the Questa Mt. on the left, we followed the carreta track, and after five leagues halt, drink tisto at a hacienda near Lake Apoyo, one of those deep chasms or trous evidently former craters. On the rocks round shores of this lake are some rude Indian drawings. From a tree by the hacienda we had a capital view of the lake Managua, the promontory of Chiltepec, and the extraordinary deep blue waters of the salt lake upon it; beyond the mountains of province of Segovia. Through more half-cleared woods, narrow paths; and our guide points out what he calls a *tigre* among the brushwood; but it is probably the effect of his vivid imagination. Arrive at Managua. The poor woman who disturbed our slumbers when last here is dead and buried. We are the only people at the Fonda. The canoe had arrived before us, and all our traps are safe at the Fonda.

Managua.
March 10, 1867.

Slept much better last night than I have for some time. The Carib boy Thomas had been dissipating, and was consequently seedy this morning. Although the large wash-tub had been used to mix lime for whitewash in, still we made shift to use it, as a good bath is indeed a rare luxury here. Bells ringing away here pretty strong, but not so overwhelming as at Leon. After noon our courtyard, where the cockpit is, is crowded with the rank, fashion, rag, tag, and bobtail of Managua, and cockfighting, betting, quarrelling, shouting, &c. are carried on, greatly to the prejudice of a peaceful Sabbath. This hullabaloo lasts until sunset, when the crowds gradually draw off in groups, carrying with them their dead and wounded combatant cocks. In the evening, having loaded the canoe as low in the water as it would well float,

we despatch it, with the Caribs in it and.Julio, for San Ubaldo *viá*
Tipitapa. Julio has orders to land at San Ubaldo, where an anvil for
Javali has to be left, and come up to Libertad. More processions of Saints,
in hopes of extinguishing the cholera, still prevalent here. A letter Captain
Pim had wrote to Dr. Seemann from here on the 28th ult. is brought back,
the courier being afraid? (as it was stated) to pass Libertad on account of
the cholera there being bad (this last fact is afterwards found to be quite
false). A new lad, Ezekiel Silva, is engaged as mozo to Captain Pim; and
a mule, small, but not bad for fifteen dollars, on which the mozo is to ride,
carrying the maleta, &c. Slept badly.

Managua viá *Pasquiel to Ranche Pedro.*
March 11, 1867.

Rising at 4 o'clock A.M., we find Prospero punctual with his chocolate;
and our new mozo expeditious in saddling the animals, which, with our
blankets on the saddles, with hammocks and alforeas, look more picturesque
than imposing. We have a pretty shady ride. Plenty of monkeys (*Cebus
albifrons*) enlivening the road. Pass at least seven streams, all of whose
waters are noxious. Halfway to Tipitapa we met Julio, who had lost his
blanket, and was walking from Tipitapa, where the canoe had arrived, back
to Managua for it. We turned him back (if he had gone into town and
back he would have had a walk of 48 miles; nothing to him, for these Nicaraguans are number-one pedestrians), and he easily kept up with our mules.
Arriving at Tipitapa, we leave Julio to bring on the boy from Granada, with
saddle, to Pasquiel; and the canoe is transported by carreta to the same place.
We ride on to the Rancho of Pasquiel Hacienda, crossing the Panaloya by
the same bridge, beneath the Falls. At first the people of Pasquiel were
rather surly; but a nip of something neat opened their eyes, and we enjoyed
a good breakfast; after which we waited for the canoe and saddle, both of
which were late. At 3 P.M. the canoe came on the carreta, and in launching
a piece of her stern was knocked off. Whilst this operation is proceeding
some Vacqueros are lassoing cattle close by, and I have a good opportunity
of watching their prowess. Just as we were starting off Captain Pim's saddle
and bridle arrive from Granada, which are put on the little horse of his that
I ride, and are most comfortable. Night coming on, we lose the track several
times, and put into Pedro? instead of proceeding to the Rio Malagatoya.
Our route now led over flat plains, the marshy ground of which was now
caked with the heat. Numerous herds of cattle were in vain seeking for
pasture, and at convenient spots heaps of logwood (called Brazil-wood, and
used for dyeing) were collected. We put up quail, and there were plenty
of snake-birds (*jacanas*), their lemon-coloured underwing contrasting with
the deep brown of their plumage. We had to sling our hammocks in a
deserted rancho or hut.

Ranche Pedro to Pedro Blanco.
March 12, 1867.

Accustomed, as we are, to turning out by star or moonlight, still it is
always a trying operation; but circumstances are inexorable, and we have to
accomplish the distance lost yesterday. We are soon off and on the plain;
but "more haste less speed," and we lose our track, and are two good cool
hours before we get into the highway (such a way as it is) to the Malaga-

toya river. We strike the river higher up than we ought, and breakfast off venison. Bathe in the river, which is very dry at this season, between deep banks; its stream when flooded must be dangerous. Quantities of parroquets and macaws, with parrots, abound. Our ride is now rocky, and the stones and basalt rocks play the very —— with our unshod animals. Scenery more wooded and undulating. We pass through several well-cleared avenues, and finally, after a hot march through the heat of the day, arrive by sundown at Don Sebastian Marengo's Hacienda, where we have dinner, and, for a wonder, are not charged for the said meal. Push on after dinner, and reach Pedro Blanco by moonlight. Sling our hammocks, and to sleep. Very cold, as we are now a slight height above the lake, and there is no protection against the winds, only the roof of dried grass.

Over country called Jicaral, from being overgrown with Jicara trees (*Crescentia cujete*, or calabash-tree). These trees are cultivated for obtaining calabash fruit, from the rind of which bowls, bottles, &c. are made.

We met here, for the first time, what is called a Jicaral, or tract of land overgrown by jicara trees. It is quite a characteristic feature in the country, and must be described in a few words. The tree is the *Crescentia cujete*, or calabash-tree, well known by the use which is made of the hard shell of its fruit in manufacturing vessels for domestic purposes. The drinking-cups constructed from a smaller species, of an oval form, are called jicaras; while the bowls or basins prepared from a large variety, of a compressed subglobular shape, sometimes of as much as one foot in diameter, are named guacales. For the purpose of manufacturing these vessels the tree is cultivated. Here, however, I am speaking of the wild tree, which bears fruit of the size of the large orange. The tree is small, with a number of long, thin, worm-shaped branches, covered all along with small and very poor leaves of their own, but bearing an additional vegetation of Bromeliaceæ, in tufts of stiff leaves, striped red and green, in parrot-like colours, so that a superficial observer may believe these tufts to be the flowers of the tree. To form an idea of a Jicaral a number of these trees must be imagined scattered over a horizontal portion of the country, the soil of which consists of a black stiff clay, and which is so situated as to become overflowed in the rainy season, when the entire district is transformed into a marsh. The plains abound in small armadillos, across which we came continually, whilst now and then packs of *coyotes*, a small species of wild wolf-like dog, would be seen. During the dry season the soil becomes nearly as hard as stone, and cracked in all directions, so that it is sometimes exceedingly rough, and, with its dark colour, appears almost like a field of lava. Between the trees some tufts of a coarse kind of grass, and bushes of the *Aroma mimosa*, with sweet-scented yellow catkins, are scattered. The ground under the trees is strewed with the fruits, which are eagerly sought and eaten by the cattle, the succulent pulp allaying at the same time their hunger and thirst. The skeletons of cows, horses, and mules lying about form an essential feature of an extended Jicaral, as a considerable number of these animals die in such localities from want of food and water during the dry season. A region of Jicarals on a large scale extends all along the foot of the tablelands of Chontales, Matagalpa, and New Segovia. In this plain country are here and there knolls with clumps of spiny cactuses with flattened pear-shaped joints and scarlet fruit, small prickly palms, and bull's-horn thorn (a bipinnate acacia), always swarming with fiery little ants (*Pseudomyrma bicolor*), besides a quantity of the shrub with dangerous sharp curved horns, called "*Viena paraca*," (*i. e.* "come here") by the Mestizos.

Pedro Blanco to Juigalpa.

March 13, 1867.

By break of day we are up and doing, and ride to breakfast at San Nicolas, passing pretty uplands, feeding-pastures, and grazing-country. Palms. Species of espadillo (*Yucca*) in bloom. Bamboo * and small bamboo (palmita) with calabash-trees abound. Latter have few small twigs, the leaves growing out of the larger branches, and the calabashes from the greater limbs. This tree seems also subject more than other to parasitic plants, orchids, &c. Fortunately we had a good tongue in our alforcas, which enabled us to breakfast well at San Nicolas. The cactus grows on some trees, looking like so many twisted green snakes and iguanas writhing about the stem. Go down to a brook near San Nicolas to bathe. Walk. Red-hatted woodpecker † and humming-birds. Fish striped like perch in the pools. After a rugged ride, arrive at Juigalpa, quite ready for our dinner, at which the tongue again performed good service, backed up by the universal frijöles and eggs. Captain Pim's stirrup leather, which is broken, is here mended, and we turn into our hammocks to receive visitors, including the Deputy of Chontales. Sketch. During the night a cow in the verandah kept lowing for her calf, lately defunct; and in the next house a midnight mass for the dead or dying sounded mournfully, as the chanting of the priests kept us awake till early morning.

Juigalpa to Libertad.

March 14, 1867.

Leave Juigalpa by 5 o'clock, and pass through lovely scenery, grassy and park-like slopes, by the side of the river fine shady trees similar to the horse-chestnut (*Cedrela*). Well-watered country, and from the heights good distant views of Mombacho mountain. Buy some venison on the way, killed last night. There is a long rise over some hilly pass ; and here we are passed by some ruffianly-looking fellows, who are just in time to take possession of the hut, where we intend breakfasting, before we get there. Halt at a hut on the pass about 1000 feet above the lake, La Puerta by name. Captain Pim and self go down a steep pass on the face of a perpendicular rock to an old Indian well, where a calabash-bath is refreshing. The fresh venison turns out first rate at breakfast, and, with milk and coffee, feel luxurious. Ascend ridge of mountains, passing the northern shoulder. The glens filled with miniature bamboo. Gorgeous autumnal tints on the trees. Flank the high range of mountains (Alto Grande), whose peaks rise like the battlements of Titanic castles, with embrasures, pinnacles, &c. Shoot a brace of quail. Pass Indian tumuli lately opened. Ancient stone pillar from interior of one formerly upright in centre. Tumuli built up of stone. Arrive at Libertad, and go to Wolfe's store. Put up at Mrs. Booley's, an American woman of peculiar prejudices and many corns.

---

* The so-called Bamboo of Central America is not the true *Bambusa* of India, but an allied genus of the *Bambusaceae*, including the *Guaduas* and the *Chusqueas*: besides, the word Bamboo is applied indifferently to *Arundinarias* nearly everywhere.

† *Centrurus Puckeraui.*

Libertad viâ *Tigre Mine to Javali.*

March 15, 1867.

Visit Wolfe and De Barruel, the storekeepers. Bathe in the Rio Mico's muddy stream. Meet Paul Giraud, who has ascended the Mico from Bluefields. His information hazy and incorrect. Start off after breakfast—a large party, Wolfe, Barruel, Captain Pim, Giraud, Mrs. Booley, and self—for Tigre Mine, the property of some Frenchmen. Road rather bad. Examine the quartz and ore works, tramway and mill. See some good samples of ore crushed and washed. Leave Mrs. Booley at the mine; and Captain Pim and self, with guide, go on by Barbicalli road towards Javali. Green long whip-snake. Horrid bad road, worst I have ever seen, Madagascar hardly excepted; mud up to the mule's ears. Wading, climbing, scrambling, and fagging, we are hours getting to El Cedro. Here we drink some chicha, or native beer made from maize; and get a better guide, who takes us by a machete road through the forest, a short cut to Javali mine. Meet Dr. Seemann, and am kindly received by Colonel and Mrs. Maury at their house, built of cedar planks, close by the mills, which follow the course of the stream dammed up above. Water power for five mills. The top mill is a turbine, second a horizontal, and a vertical overshoot next; below are two horizontal. The noise of the water-wheels is unceasing, and their creaking is not unlike the sound of an Indian singing.

Javali Gold-mine.

March 16, 1867.

Wash below the water-wheels, and see the native labourers paid and receive their token for rations; they carry the ore in ox-hide bags, the strap of which passes round their foreheads: they have to carry so many loads per diem, and are well paid. Make a sketch of the works[*], and send clothes to be washed. Take my gun and wander through the woods of Pavone, looking for game; see plenty of small birds of brilliant plumage (trogons, flycatchers, motmots, humming-birds), and butterflies, snakes, and squirrels: no game. In the evening walk with Mrs. Maury and her little boy Matthew. Mr. Wickham, who has been up the Blewfields river, comes over from San Domingo to see Capt. Pim. We had a jollification in the evening and improvised dance.

" On the 16th of March I had the pleasure of welcoming at the mine my friends Captain Bedford Pim, R.N., and his travelling companion, Lieut. Oliver, R.A. Their arrival was made the occasion of a nocturnal fête, such as had, up to that time, never been witnessed in those parts. By the natives it was thought truly splendid. After all our people and as many of their friends as they liked to invite had partaken of a hot supper and as much grog as they wished to drink, some fireworks which one of our men had contrived were displayed before the principal house, and some transparencies with inscriptions complimentary to the guests lit up. After that a band of music, vile beyond description, but absolutely charming in the opinion of the natives, struck up; and dancing (such dancing!) was kept up till an early hour. I don't think that Captain Pim altogether thanked me for having permitted the fête, as the natives were perhaps rather too demonstrative in expressing over

---

[*] See view given as frontispiece in ' *Dottings on the Roadside, in Panama, Nicaragua, and Mosquito,*' by Pim and Seemann.

and over again their gratitude to him for having done so much for their country as he has done. Fond as he would have been to move about freely amongst the gay scene, he had to sit indoors nearly all night to escape hearing his praises *ad nauseam* shouted into his ears.

" At this nocturnal fête there were several pure Indians, amongst them the son of the one who had shown the Javali for three cows, and who was then working on the mine."—Dr. Seemann's ' *Dottings,*' p. 203.

A short time afterwards a melancholy event occurred at the mines, resulting in the death of James Skewes, head carpenter. Skewes, who was a native of Camborne, accompanied the doctor of the mines to visit a patient at Acoyapa. On their way back they fell in with Captain White, who is a native of St. Ives, Cornwall, an agent of Chontales Mines. He was accompanied by a miner named Piper, a native of Helston. All were on horseback, but some were better mounted than others; and on Captain White's leaving Piper in the rear deceased remonstrated with him. Angry words followed, and a challenge to fight ensued. Four rounds were fought, and White went to the ground each time. He then drew his revolver and shot Skewes, the ball passing through the right lung. The only witness to the tragic event was the doctor, who did all that he could for the unfortunate man, but his aid was of no avail, deceased expiring in about twenty minutes. White, on reaching the mine, gave himself up to the English Consul. He was taken to Libertad, and was afterwards taken to Juigalpa, where he awaited his trial. Deceased was formerly a member of the Camborne Rifle corps, and was highly respected. He left Camborne about two years ago, as head carpenter of the Chontales Mines, which important post he filled to the entire satisfaction of the company.

Javali, San Domingo. Ascend Peña Blanca.

March 17, 1867.

After an early breakfast ride out to San Domingo mine, the head-quarters of the Chontales Gold and Silver Mining Company. Here are plenty of English, American, and Cornish miners &c. Examine the sites for inclined planes and the large water-wheel which is to work eight cups. Ride on to Consuelo mine, and ascend the summit of Peña Blanca, from which a distant view over primitive forest away into Mosquito territory is obtained and all the mountains. Ometepec bears 29° and Madera 20° W. of south by compass. Return to Javali. Cocktails all the order of the day at San Domingo.

Javali and San Domingo Mines.

March 18, 1867.

Walk up to Pollock's tunnel and Griffin's shaft with Dr. Seemann, who is a brother-in-law of Capt. Anderson of our brigade. Walk then to San Domingo mine, and take a panoramic view of the whole works. Back to Javali. Meet Mrs. Robinson, Mrs. Paul, and Mrs. Simmons at breakfast at San Domingo. Cocktails as usual.

Javali Mine to Libertad.

March 19, 1867.

Breakfast tolerably early. Receive Capt. Pim's last instructions, and take leave of Col. and Mrs. Maury and Dr. Seemann &c. Start off with Capt. Pim

and Mr. Melzer, and examine the site of the proposed new town. Two of the hired mules were missing, so I left Julio to bring them on with the baggage, and, taking leave of Capt. Pim, rode with Mr. Melzer to his clearing, where I left him, taking with me a soft sandy-haired little sloth, with fierce claws and sleepy head and long tongue. He was placed in the holster, but before reaching Libertad was quite dead. Rode on alone through the forest by the Company's road, which was bad enough, but much superior to Barbicelli's road. Stopped at the Company's house at the Pital, where the forest ends and the plains begin, and delivered a letter to and spoke with a certain Leon Celerio, who is to accompany me as interpreter at $20 a month if I think fit. I do not think him fit, however, and so do not engage him. Arrived before dark at Libertad and saw Mr. Wolfe, who is to provide the cargo, bullocks, and stores for the cutting; I find that the animals and stores, but no men, are forthcoming. Skinned the sloth before dinner. Put up at Mrs. Booley's. Before turning in for the night I asked the woman who helps in the hut to examine my feet, and she forthwith proceeded to extract from my feet a disgusting chigoe, which had been long enough undiscovered to spread considerably before being ejected. In the evening Julio arrives from Javali with the traps, but there are still two oxen and three men not forthcoming.

Libertad to Ranche of Esquipula.

March 20, 1867.

By breakfast-time the two expected oxen arrived, and I sent back by their bearer a note to Capt. Pim at Javali. My experience of bullock-driving now commences. One driver is with difficulty engaged, taken before the magistrate, a dirty, naked native, lying in a dark room on an ox-hide bed. Our first recruit is called Francisco Perez, and is engaged at $12 a month. Meantime some of the oxen get away, and have to be brought back; next Ezekiel says he is lame and cannot walk, he must ride; whilst Julio has a severe toothache, and shows signs of discontent. It is fortunate that I cannot understand what they say, as I escape their importunities. Another wild-looking Indian is secured as a driver and duly matriculated; and as the saddler, who promised to have my saddle completed by this morning, has not touched it, I have to content myself with a common alborda. After dinner we make a start. At first go off one bull without a cargo disappears at full pace, the others kick off their cargoes and disperse in various directions outside the town, and all of us after them; at least an hour elapses before all, except one, are secured, their cargoes repacked, only to be interrupted by similar scenes till dark, when they are more quiet and fatigued, and we travel steadily at a foot's pace for three leagues to a ranche belonging to the Company at Esquipula, where we arrive about midnight under a bright moon, and, sleeping on a feather bed, soon forget where I am or how I got there.

Ranche, Esquipula, to Acoyapa.

March 21, 1867.

Breeze continually blows through middle of the day. A thick fog covered the landscape. Rouse up the but too sleepy hirelings with the cattle and cargoes. I and Ezekiel wait for a cup of coffee and breakfast kindly supplied by Mrs. King: plenty of milk, bread and butter, and fowl. Start off, catch up the oxen, who are not progressing fast, and some of which already show signs of lameness. We now descend easy passes along the Company's road;

pieces of machinery for San Domingo lie scattered here and there, and several broken axles &c. of carretas attest the difficulty of transport in this country. I met a Mr. George Griffin in the Company's service, who is anxious to obtain employment on the proposed railway. I ride on so as to avoid the noonday sun, and reach Acoyapa at 11.30 A.M., meeting Señor Don Dolores Bermudez, whose comfortable house is on the N.W. corner of the Plaza opposite a guard-house. Señor Bermudez talks English well, has been to the States, and is altogether in advance of his countrymen. His wife sits at table with him at meals &c. Catch a nasty cold by lying in a hammock in a draught when perspiring. Meet De Barruel on his way from San Ubaldo to Libertad. The oxen do not come in till 3 P.M., and then two of them very lame. Arrival of a number of pressed recruits, amongst whom soon after a case of cholera is reported; the reputed case is instantly dismissed to his friends, and calmness is restored to the excited population. In the evening the new President's proclamation of amnesty is read in public at each corner, with music, rockets (home-made), and in the evening a dance, to which my host and hostess go dressed in the height of fashion, whilst I retire to bed very soon after 9 o'clock.

Acoyapa to Hacienda, Madroños.

March 22, 1867.

Up at early dawn, as is, indeed, getting customary to me; and it is certainly the most charming time in this hot climate. Pay Bermudez $2 for forage for the beasts; he refuses to charge me for my board &c. Leave cargo of one lame bullock behind with Bermudez. Send on the beasts a short way, whilst I wait for a cup of chocolate; then soon catching them up, I find to my dismay that Torribilio has bolted, and instead of the expected four only one is with me, and who knows when he intends to bolt. The oxen travel but slowly, so on reaching the river Ojo quapa we bivouac, cook chocolate and a tin of beef, and swing in my hammock till it is cool enough to proceed. Before our meal I shot a couple of *lapas* or macaws, which were pronounced good to eat, and forthwith disappeared before the appetites of my followers. I also bought some jerked beef for 3½ reales from a passer-by in case our party should fail in food. This river, according to Julio, runs into the lake at Nanzital. Another party from the opposite direction halt at the same time, and we exchange civilities, he presenting me with quebada cheese, and I biscuit and cognac to him. Another young man joins our party, who, appearing willing to come to the piquet, I engage and set him to work at once, his name being Pietro Palacios. A little further on we come across a lot of monkeys, when I shot an old coxoo, or black-skinned, black-faced monkey (*Mycetes palliatus*); and I felt quite sorry when I had done so, as some little ones looked down on me till I felt very guilty. Pass large hacienda of Vera Cruz, and through some wild deserted country pass a cross to commemorate a murder in this lonely spot. Attacked by wasps; Julio stung. On by night after dark; halt at Madroños.

Hacienda, Madroños, to Rancho, Tenayasapa.

March 23, 1867.

By moonlight early despatched the oxen and cargoes, with Julio, towards Aminas, whilst I snatched another hour's sleep, and then had a bathe in a neighbouring brook kindly shown me by Rufina Baez, one of the civilest

Nicaraguans I have met. A nice cloudy morning. 14 dimes was the charge for every thing. Pretty scenery; on the left La Bentana mountain raised its head, and on the right to the south Mount Anon, with basaltic rocks on the summit beyond the heights of Memeltepee. Señor Baez accompanied us some way himself on our journey. He informed me that there was a gold mine close by Vera Cruz which he wished examined; he had no samples of quartz or gold to show. We caught the oxen up, after a couple of long leagues, close by Animas, a large hacienda, there being some 7000 head of cattle on the estate. All this country is pretty level, the hills detached and smooth. I had a letter from Acoyapa for Juan Lopez, the steward at Animas; but when I presented it he was not at all gracious. However, I had breakfast there, and let the oxen go on to the river Del Animas, whence, on consulting Julio, I think of reaching San Miguel late to-night, as it appears practicable. Accordingly I give Julio $1 and 6 dimes for subsistence, and ride off across the plains, feeling the heat of the sun almost intolerable. A long day's ride through plain, hill, and dale; more palms and bamboos appearing, crowds of cattle and many ranches and haciendas. We miss our way several times and are set right, till after nightfall we become regularly fixed in some bamboo thickets; and after some scrambling we gave it up as a bad job, and went back to the last rancho for a guide. No one, however, would go till morning, so we slept there in the open air after a tin of preserved mutton and biscuit; a wild unbroken mule on one side, and cows, whose offspring are railed in, wandering around and snuffing at one.

Tenayasapa to San Miguelito. Hall.

March 24, 1867.

Slept most uncomfortably, or rather not at all; the blanket wet with dew, and clothes covered with garrapatas which vied successfully with the mosquitoes in keeping me awake. At daylight aroused Ezekiel, and refreshed myself with milk (a draught of this in a guacal), which was being poured from buckets into a large wooden trough, the milk so strong and creamy as to require water with it to bring it to drinking consistency. A flock of parroquets kept up a loud chorus from their roosting-place above my head. Started in mist from the ranche, with the master as a guide; taking a more southerly course we struck a good road through dense *vinea brava* (bamboo) thickets, whence we viewed a deer and crossed the river Ayasapa. Piraguas ascending this river as far up as this, we now crossed extensive savannah nearly all burnt up, bitterns here and there, and cattle looming through the dense fog. The baguses seemed very long, and when the fog cleared and the guide declared our road was straight ahead, I gave him the *una peso* demanded and rode on; but, on reaching the woods beyond the savannah, found that the paths, diverging again, placed us in doubt; but a vacquero kindly put us in the road, when we reached the river El Camastro, where a bridge of three or four bamboos only forced our animals to swim across. More woods, and then swampy burnt marshes and bad travelling till we reached a ranche, where more milk was acceptable; as the sun was getting high and the fog had long cleared up. Another league of wood and swamp brought us to San Miguelito again, where I found Mr. Griffiths alone in his glory, and was very glad of a good breakfast, wash, &c., and laid resting in the hammock till dinner. In the evening a bathe and eating oranges, whilst Capt. Pim's letter was despatched by canoe to the Commandant of San Carlos. Sunset behind E. flank of Madera Island.

San Miguelito.

March 25, 1867.

Rose with the sun, and bathed in the lake; my body is covered from head to foot with garrapata-bites, ant-bites, &c., and the irritation is excessive. Shot a cock and hen prairie-fowl (*Tinamus* sp.); saw squirrel and nest. Breakfast pretty good. After breakfast shot a macaw, as Griffiths wanted its feathers. The rest of the morning filling cartridges with No. 6 shot and B. B. for the cutting. No Julio with the oxen yet. Instructed the boy Ezekiel in filling cartridges till 1 P.M., when a cocktail revived me. Thermometer 89° in the shade. My health and spirits both good, in spite of the reverse to an agreeable companion. After dinner ride off with Ezekiel, gun in hand, to look for venison; come back after dark without success—only a prairie-fowl. My mule bolts and throws me close by the hut. Find Julio, who appears to have been drinking, and to have left the oxen knocked up at various places along the road. 'My shirt torn and side cut by fall. The natives call the prairie-fowl *Chacaluca.*

San Miguelito.

March 26, 1867.

Did not sleep well from the effects of mosquitoes and garrapata-bites. Up by moonlight before sunrise, and shoot three prairie-fowls (chacalacas), but see no deer. Back very hot, and drink milk from Chico's opposite, chocolate, &c. Despatch off Julio and Ezekiel, the former to Acoyapa on the hired mule, and the latter to bring up the cargoes and oxen. Send a letter to Bermudez, instructing him to buy an ox to bring in the cargo left behind. Bathe. Give Julio $2 for expenses, and Ezekiel 8 dimes. Writing up journal. Took angles by compass from house at San Miguelito :—

		°
Bernadino island ...	Right tangent	302
	Left tangent	301½
Bernado island......	Right tangent	297½
	Left tangent	294
Ometepec mountain	Right tangent	275
	Centre peak.............	273
	Left tangent ...,......	271
Madera mountain ..	Right tangent	269½
	Centre peak.............	266½
	Left tangent	263½
Orosi mountain ? ...	Peak or two peaks of } 226½ -227 }	. In evening, peaks plain.
	Orosi mountain... } 222 -223 }	

The mountains of Costa Rica extraordinarily plainly visible. Make a sketch of them.

Island of Ometepec=two mountains. One of the two peaks of the island bears the name of Ometepec; the other is called the Peak of Madera. According to Baron Bulow, Ometepec has an altitude of 5100 feet, Madera an altitude of 4190 feet. The former can be ascended without difficulty. The lower region is covered with forests, the higher with savannahs. The peak of Madera is thickly wooded from the water's edge to the summit. There may be considerable difficulties in penetrating through the forest, which, as I imagine, conceals some objects of Indian antiquity. During the dry season, while for months a spotless sky is spread over Nicaragua, a thick cloud covers the top of the peak of Ometepec, and, if examined on the spot, may be observed to be in a constant process of originating on the north-eastern side of the

summit to roll over it in a direction to the south-west, where it is in an equally
constant process of dissolving. The north-eastern trade-wind striking against
the side of the mountain is forced to cross the apex, and, passing thus from
a warmer into a colder region of the atmosphere, is obliged to part with a
portion of the water held in solution. Thus the cloud is produced on the
windward side of the summit. On the lee side the reverse takes place. The
wind descends from the colder to the warmer region, where the cloud is dis-
solved, not, however, before a part of its water has collected in heavy rain-
drops, which I have observed to fall even at the northern foot of the mountain from a thin and almost transparent veil surrounding the cone. I have
already mentioned this kind of local precipitation in reference to the summit
of Mombacho. During the five days of my sojourn I never saw the summit
uncovered for a single moment. Another observation I made during this
time was that of the regular gusts of wind which poured down the side of
the mountain every evening. As to the peak of Madera, I cannot tell
whether it exhibits the same phenomenon in an equally regular manner.
From a distance, however, I have seen it capped with a similar cloud, and
this is occasionally the case with the summit of Mombacho mountain.

In the evening, just when going to bed, the cargo-bullocks come in, greatly
to my pleasure, for I had much misgiving as to the fate of the animals and
goods. Six days from Libertad.

San Miguelito.
March 27, 1867.

Bathe by the lake, and write. Stay in doors, packing &c.; reading
all day. In afternoon sketch San Miguelito, with Madera and Ometepec
in the distance. After dinner see Madera and Ometepec most plainly.
Sun sets behind Madera. Amplitude:—Magnetic bearing 265° by compass;
compass bearing of Mombacho mountain 285°; of Zapatero island 283°.
These last two, Zapatero and Mombacho, were visible plainly after sunset,
and at first I could hardly believe that I could see them. Many mosquitoes
and sand-flies; very much bitten. Bathe in evening before sunset. Thermometer 90° at 4 P.M.; very hot. Nice cool breeze in evening. Bongo men,
consisting of so many marineros under a patron, all of them coloured, are a
class on the retention of whom the President depends; there are, perhaps,
from 600 to 800 on the lake, and are the pluckiest of the inhabitants; can
turn the scale of a revolution in the country.

San Miguelito. Bivouac.
March 28, 1867.

Glorious scene of distant mountains disappeared. Start for the cutting
by moonlight. The lake appears a boundless ocean to the eye. Bathe in
the lake, if, indeed, it can be called bathing where one cannot comfortably
go out further from the shore than a yard or two, and not deeper than
one's knees, for fear of alligators and sharks, *guapotes*, &c. Whilst on shore
the jigger is always on the look out for any naked feet in which it may find a
permanent home. Breakfast being over, we start off under a hot sun, with
the following party, viz. self, Eusebio, guide (a Spaniard), and five men
(tall Costa Rican, Chicot Libertad, Chicot Perez, Gregorio, surnamed Chopin,
and a young *muchacho*). A bull and an ox with cargoes; a bull for slay-
ing; and a grey horse with cargo. I ride the fifteen-dollar mule. At first

we do not follow the line already boned out (laid down), as the ground is too marshy to admit of our heavily-loaded animals to pass with safety; therefore, making a slight circuit to the north, we pass slightly broken and undulating ground skirting the marshy lagoon, and by savannah- and bamboo-thickets strike the cutting in a grove of *Coroso* palms, by a scanty but valuable puddle of water. This is reported by the guide as the last we should meet with; we therefore unload the beasts, letting them take their fill and graze. Shooting at a chacalaca, the report of my gun aroused a deer, which was allowed to pass unscathed.

On journey through Cutting. *No. I. Rancho. Bivouac.*
March 29, 1867.

Early daylight awaited by me with feverish eagerness; my face and hands swollen beyond recognition by mosquito-bites. Wet and dark, with heavy dews. I bathe in the long wet grass; but there is no water to drink, till I find Eusebio has economically reserved a few mouthfuls of muddy water for himself and me. We now leave the savannah and all traces of civilization, entering the real bush about the same spot where Col. Cauty commenced his. This, a mere path cut with machetes through the forest, ordinary sized trees that prevent the proper boning out of the line being cut by axe; but any enormous trees that would require a day's labour are avoided, the line diverging on their account. Wherever trees have fallen across the track, although the boning is carried on straight, a path for animals is cut round to avoid it; similarly, where the ground over which the line passes is too rough or steep, as it often is, for the pack-mules &c. to pass, a path for them diverges sometimes for a considerable distance to enable their passage. About 10 A.M. we found a path leading to a camping-ground with a small pool of water, although it was muddied by dung of mountain-cow &c. Here we stopped for a meal. Meantime I had shot three guans and two pavones, so we had no lack of food. The pavones, or curassows, are magnificent birds; the male black, with yellow excrescence, white belly, and black crest; female brown, and mottled white-and-black crest. Saw a snake. Woods very dry. Shoot another pavon, making six turkeys in all. I ride on in advance, so as to have best chance of game; but, on account of the slow progression of the oxen, am unable to get on at all quickly. Plenty of monkeys follow, brown (*Ateles*) and black ones. About 4 P.M. come to a small stream, where I find a letter from Collinson and a rancho. Light a fire ready for the remainder of party to cook by when they come. The cargoes do not arrive till nearly dark, and so we have to wait the night here. When waiting for the party to arrive I was attracted by a flannel shirt torn in shreds and hung upon a tree, as if to mark something, at a slight distance off in the wood; my curiosity being awakened, I went up to it, and underneath, covered with dead leaves, was a portmanteau, or rather the remains of one, partially ransacked. This portmanteau had been left behind in the rancho, and, on the rancho being deserted, the monkeys had evidently from curiosity dragged the portmanteau out, ransacked its contents, and then deposited it where I found it.

Reach Camp No. XIV. of Cutting-party.
March 30, 1867.

Start off early on my mule quite alone, leaving the cargoes and men to follow as quickly as possible under Eusebio. All the country is densely wooded, here and there monstrous trees fallen from age and covered with lichens, mosses, &c. Country very hilly and in parts almost formidable. Dry watercourses, but little water; at last come to a river of size, with very steep, almost per-

pendicular banks; here I have to unload my mule, take off saddle and alforcas, and with great difficulty, after several failures, manage to get him across: another bend of the river, and I find traces of party in front in shape of baggage left behind; and further on, by a deep bend of same stream (Toolie river?), find a dead bullock swollen in the stream, and a crowd of zopilotes, vultures, turkey buzzards, and carrion-birds of various sorts. Plenty of monkeys. Shoot a guan. Sound of the " *Campanero* " or bell-bird, like two strokes on a silver bell at intervals. Meet Simon and two others of the party returning to bring on the stores left behind. About 1.30 P.M. come upon Deering, with his level ; and here, after a drink of tea and a few minutes' walk, I arrive at their camp No. XIV., situate in a deep valley between two steep hills on the banks of a watercourse, in which only pools and slightly trickling springs fill a small portion. Collinson is out. Camp presents a picturesque appearance : each man's mosquito-bar is spread on four sticks ; two tents ; fire and stores in admirable confusion. Collinson arrives before dark, and is soon followed by his Caribs, who come in whooping and screeching in capital spirits.

To explain what had occurred in our absence, we must revert to Mr. Collinson's narrative, as thus recounted by him :—

" After a laborious ascent of the river, I was landed at the village of San Miguelito with my small party. Commencing work on Monday, February 25th, through the stunted undergrowth that clothes the shores of the lake, and which swarms with gallapatos, those terrible pests of the Tropics, we proceeded with great rapidity, and, on March 1st, had so far advanced, that it was advisable to pitch our first camp. That night we swung our hammocks for the first time in the open air, and, in spite of mosquitos, slept well.

" On Tuesday, the 5th, we entered the forest, which extended from there without break, eastward, to the ocean. Up to that time we had been traversing the savannahs which skirt round the borders of the lake, and lie inland in places for many miles. These savannahs are immense plains, sometimes slightly undulating with hillocks clothed with trees standing up, at intervals, like islands in the long grass, which will often overtop the heads of the horsemen. In crossing these savannahs, and for some time after entering the forest, we suffered dreadfully from want of water, and were only too grateful to obtain any dregs that might be left in the pools frequented by the Dantes or Tapirs (*Elasmotherium bairdi* or *Tapirus bairdi*), and used by them alike for drinking and bathing.

" We could trace the commencement of Cauty's old piquete on entering the forest ; but, as I soon found it inclining too much to the southward, I decided to quit it and strike out an independent line.

" Friday, the 8th, one of my men, who had been despatched on Wednesday to San Miguelito for provisions, arrived with a welcome supply; but what we needed most was water; and had it not been for a large vine (" Bejuca "), which seems planted by Providence in dry regions, where alone it flourishes, and which yields on being cut a moderate supply of wholesome clear water, our sufferings would have been unbearable.

" The forest now began to take a more distinct character, as, intermixed with the everlasting palms, india-rubber trees, sapodillas, cedars, and, further on, mahoganies occurred in magnificent groves, sprawling their enormous roots over acres of ground, and rearing their vast height from the jungle beneath almost, as it seemed, up to the clouds.

" Tuesday, the 12th, I shot four guans (*Penelope*), the smallest species of turkey inhabiting the American forests. The country now became more broken up, our course crossing several spurs of a high range, running to the north of us, west and east.

CUTTING THROUGH PRIMÆVAL FOREST.
NICARAGUA.

" Mr. Deering began to feel the effects of drinking the filthy water we had been obliged to put up with. On Saturday, the 15th, however, greatly to our joy, we came on a watercourse with several large and clear pools.

" Monday, the 18th, we crossed the first running stream since leaving San Miguelito, and on the following day three Caribs, whom I had requested Captain Pim to send me from Leon, arrived—one of whom, Perry by name, an elderly man, I installed as " Boss " of the party.

" Our total distance up to leaving off work on Saturday afternoon was 17½ miles, in 24 working days; not so bad, taking into consideration the small number of hands. But now, having had a fair opportunity of comparing the work of these Caribs with that of the Mosquito and Woolwa Indians, employed on my first expedition, I must say that the latter were by far the best workmen. There were two very serious drawbacks to the Caribs: firstly, they were excessively particular about their food and personal comforts; if they had not for every meal plenty of meat, dampers, and vegetables well cooked, there was always great grumbling and an attempt to shirk work; they also insisted on having blankets and mosquito-bars for the night, which increased the bulk of our loads very seriously; and, secondly, they always have some man among them, generally the biggest and laziest, whose dictum is invariably followed in the blindest and most obstinate manner—reasoning is wasted on them. The Indians, on the contrary, though they certainly complain if not kept well filled, are content with any thing as long as they have sufficient of it to create a sense of repletion. When provisions were not plentiful, they would often sit up all night boiling and eating eboe-nuts (*Dipteryx oleifera*), which quite satisfied them if they could obtain enough. As for wardrobe it was all carried in the shape of a small cloth round the loins. Their respect for a white man is very great, and the virtue of obedience is rarely questioned by them.

" The country which we had passed through, nowhere in our course attaining a greater height than 400 feet above the level of the lake, had for the last few miles been broken up a good deal by isolated hills; but, on Thursday the 28th, we crossed a considerable plain, stretching, as far as the eye could reach, to our north, and bounded on our south at a distance of 5 or 6 miles by the spur of a range running north-east and south-west, which we crossed on Saturday, at a height of 716·94 feet above the lake, and at a distance of 21 miles 528 yards from San Miguelito.

" On that same day in the evening, on coming into camp, I was gladdened by finding that Lieutenant Oliver, R.A., had arrived with four men, a mule, and two bullocks laden with provisions. Mr. Oliver, at my request, volunteered to remain with us and give his valuable assistance to the expedition. As an instance of the difficulty in travelling through this country I may state that Mr. Oliver started with six bullocks, lightly laden, only two of which arrived, the rest dying on the way.

" In the morning one of my men shot a wari (*Dicotyles jacaçu*), the first large animal which had fallen a prey to us; we had shot a few turkeys before, but it was remarkable how much less game there was in the country than formerly. No animals seemed to be plentiful now, except jaguars. The natives accounted for the phenomenon in this wise:—Two years ago a terrific hurricane, similar to the one which has recently devastated St. Thomas and Tortola, swept over the country, utterly destroying Blewfields, and laying low vast tracts of the forests. The wild animals and birds were destroyed by myriads, and sought refuge in the very roads and houses of the little clearings on the coast of the ocean and the lake, where they were killed by the inhabitants. Since then hunting has become a profitless employment; but the jaguars, too hardy and cunning to be destroyed by the same means

as the other game, have grown bolder and more ferocious, attacking men wherever they meet them, and even taking the town of Blewfields by storm. I was assured, by most credible witnesses, that while we were in the cutting seventeen jaguars marched into that place one morning, and frightened the inhabitants so much by their numbers and appearance, that they shut themselves up in their houses while the jaguars killed every goat in the place—the only animals kept on the Mosquito coast."

Halt. Camp No. XIV.
March 31, 1867.

Much better from effect of three pills and a good night's rest; go down the stream a short way and bathe. Shoot a curassow; also what at first I took to be a racoon, called by the natives *quasje*, by the Spaniards *pisoti*[*]. It was very bold, coming down a tree to snarl and growl at me; a charge of BB shot soon put a stop to this, however, and his flesh was by no means despicable. The bull I had brought was killed this morning, and turned into jerked beef, strips of its flesh being salted and dried in sun, and smoked by night. As usual, make our meals from curassow, which birds eat remarkably like English turkey. The guans are not in such good condition, much smaller birds besides. Mr. Deering suffers from a recurrence of the fever, of which he is a continual victim. Before midday only the cargoes under Eusebio arrive, and an inspection of stores &c. takes place. In the evening Collinson and I walk with our guns down the watercourse, and return before dark with a brace of guans. In the evening consult the plan plotted out up to yesterday's date; decide on course for ensuing week &c.

Camp No. XV.
April 1, 1867.

Up as soon as light, and in search of game; have to content myself with one guan. Pass fresh tracks of tapir, their footmarks, and dung, &c. Join Deering in levelling till breakfast; after which I go on in front, shoot a chacalaca and a plump partridge. Squall comes on with a few drops of rain. Curious effect of wind in the forest: sound of it in the tree-tops high above one's head; and falling leaves and withered branches clattering down, whilst all below is still. Meet the cattle with baggage returning to a watercourse where there is a good pool of good water. The cutting-party come to a considerable river in front, and see a tapir. Traces of large game plentiful.

Firefly. Camp No. XVI.
April 2, 1867.

Up by misty daylight, and down the creek *solus*, shooting a brace of curassows. Every thing late in camp this morning. The cutting-party proceed; and Collinson and I going on to the river, explore down it a short way, shooting a guan and an iguana of large size. This river, which runs south, is conjectured to be either a tributary of Toolie or possibly the Indian river. On its banks are two or three unmistakable marks of machete cuts of some two seasons old, but no trace of clearing: they are evidently only remains of a hunting-party of Indians up the river after game or rubber.

At camp No. XVI. we remained the 2nd and 3rd, the working party cutting on, however, in front. Mr. Deering has fever. Our party now consisted of three

[*] *Nasua narica.* The racoon-like '*pisoti*' is very partial to iguanas, but cannot catch them very easily alone, though when in packs these *quasjes* catch them without much trouble.

Europeans, viz., Mr. Collinson, Mr. Deering, and myself, with fourteen other hands (eight Carib mahogany-cutters, under Perry the boss, a Jamaica cook, and five Spanish Americans), in all seventeen. There were three canvas tents for the men, and a mackintosh sheet stretched over a ridge covered our own three hammocks. We now experienced heavy tropical showers. At night the fire- and lantern-flies (*Lampyridæ*) were magnificent. They exhibit when at rest only two pale green lights on each side of their head; when excited or in motion the abdominal light shines bright, of a more reddish hue, and the quicker they fly the brighter the light. A lovely glowworm too, a myriapod, we saw, with two similar lights, but smaller; on being touched, a series of minute sparks like pearls scintillated down its entire length in two rows.

Firefly. Camp No. XVI.
April 3, 1867.

Do not move camp to-day, remaining at No. XVI. on account of Mr. Deering's fever, which is bad. Rain in morning. Bathe and have the only good swim I have had for a long time. I now put tobacco-juice over me, which, I find, is serviceable against the persecution of garrapatas. Shoot a curassow. Collinson takes the levelling-party, and I lay out the line in front with cutting-party. Close by the camp they find some good honey-trees, from which is extracted plenty of good, peculiarly delicately flavoured liquid honey, enough and to spare for all hands. Eaten with boiled rice, we find it very refreshing. On way to cutting shoot a *quasje* larger than last on a fine coroso palm. Fell the tree for its liquor. Breakfast brought on to us by the cook. Tea in a calabash; delicious out of a tin pannikin. Wild turkey, potted beef, flour dampers: very good living. Find no water; have recourse to large water-vines or '*bejucas*,' which, on being cut, give a tolerable supply of tasteless liquid. The natives cut off short lengths about 3 or 4 feet, and drain liquid into their mouths, holding them upright. Good long walk back to camp: have jigger taken out of toe on right foot; it has been a passenger there from San Miguel. Stuff up the hole it makes with tobacco-ashes. Bathe and swim. More tobacco-juice.

Camp XVII. Tommygoff.
April 4, 1867.

The Brown horse gives in. At daybreak a heavy downfall specimen of tropical shower causes a scramble to get the tea, flour, and sugar, and other stores under cover of our waterproof tent. Put glycerine on my sores. I am very lame from sore feet. Borrow an old pair of Collinson's boots, which are much more comfortable. Slight headache. I go on with cutting-party. See another quasje close by place where I shot one yesterday; but do not get a shot. No liquor run from palm yet. To-day we have to cut down several trees; among others, guavas. These trees have very elegant buttresses which make their trunks look larger than in reality, as the body of the tree is small. The trees are so entangled with parasites, vines and lianes, that the fall of one tree generally involves the fall of several besides, or often refuse to fall, being upheld by its companions. Pass a magnificent india-rubber tree. Sound of bird with note like shrill railway-whistle[*]. Establish Camp XVII. at water (scanty) near the immense india-rubber tree. Feet much swollen and very tired. Just before dinner they find and kill a

---

[*] This bird is the Toledo (*Chiroxiphia lineata*), a small bird about the size of a linnet, velvety black in colour, with a flat scarlet crest and sky-blue feathers on its back; its curious note is a deep-toned whistle, and it frequents the deepest woods.

' *tamaguso* ' or tommygoff snake close to our hammocks, also a large centipede on our waterproof dining-sheet. Free from mosquitoes.

March to Camp XVIII., or Deserter Camp.
April 5, 1867.

Rain again falls during the night; but we are well prepared for it. Tent well ridged down, cords slack, &c. Our tent is composed of mackintosh, and answers admirably. Our climate here among the woods and hills is quite different to the dry season near the large lakes. The ground is dry, and sucks it all in, however, like a sponge. Feet still swollen about the ankles; painful to walk. Put on tobacco-juice and glycerine. I go on to take the cutting-party, Collinson levelling not much in rear of the camp, we cutting not much in front. The ground is easier than it has been latterly and there is no precipitous climbing. Reach water before breakfast at junction of two streams. All these streams appear to run to the south, probably to the San Juan or Indian River. Come to a stiff hill, and make an angle to the south to avoid the hill. Grey horse succumbs. Back to camp on the stream. Jerked meat and dampers for dinner, and quinine by way of bitters.

Deserter Camp, or Camp XVIII.
April 6, 1867.

For a wonder, no rain last night or this morning. Good opportunity for drying our clothes. Simon goes back with the mules to camp No. XIV. to fetch up the main supply of provisions left behind there. Sugar is short, and accordingly the allowance decreased, at which there is much murmuring. Our course lies to-day parallel with or constantly cutting the river; so there is no want of water. Cut through what apparently has been an Indian clearing.

We now came across the Soupar palm (*Guilielma speciosa*), for the first time: this palm is universally grown by the Indians round their houses, and its fruit, tasting much like a yam, is boiled and eaten when ripe. The tree is about 60 feet in height, with a straight stem covered by regular bands of long black prickles, used by the natives as needles; the appearance of the leaves on the top is similar to the cabbage-palm. The existence of these palms is but very doubtful evidence of domestic habitation.

After ascending gradually for the next few days, we, to my delight, espied for the first time a grove of four eboe-trees (*Dipterix oleifera*): I took this as a certain sign of our proximity to the summit-level, as none of those trees grow on the lake and Pacific slopes of the isthmus. At the same time the vegetation, as if by magic, changed. On the lake slope the woods are principally hard and small-leaved. Mahoganies (*Swietenia mahogoni*), cedars (*Cedrela odorata*), lance-wood (*Duguetia quitarensis*), lignum vitæ (*Guaiacum officinale*), and india-rubber (*Castilloa elastica*) are distinguishing features. The jungle is exceedingly tough, in many places miles of prickly pear (*Bromelia karatas*), bamboo, with " bejucas," and vines, which tried the sharpest " machete " and strongest arm to cut; while the surface of the ground, except in the bottoms of the valleys, was arid, stony, and so heated that our feet were burnt and blistered by it; watercourses were comparatively few, and many of them dry. Such a country was quite unfamiliar to my previous experiences; but now every day the changing vegetation and aspect of the country reminded me more and more of the Mosquito coast. The vines became green and tender; the great coroso and cabbage-palms were now mixed with the swallow-tail (*Geonoma*), so useful for thatching, and ribbon-

like leaves of the *Curculigo latifolia*; while the prickly and club-rooted zanona (*Socratea*) would mingle their foliage with the locust-trees (*Hymenæa courbrail*); the entada with their mahogany seeds, and the swelling trumpet-trees (*Cecropia peltata*), sarsaparilla (*Smilax medica*), and the clinging vanilla began to appear, and the invaluable silk-grass (*Bromelia*) took the place of the prickly pear. Lovely tree-ferns gave their incomparably delicate appearance to grace the vegetation; running streams occurred more frequently, and the ground became springy and cool under our feet, while it acquired that rich black colour so suggestive of fertility.

Deserter Camp, Camp XVIII.
April 7, 1867.

A fine tapir comes and looks at us across the stream. The nipple of my rifle is foul; so I take the smooth-bore breech-loader and wound the beast, who retires precipitately, followed by self and one or two boys (Caribs). I find blood and traces of the animal; but after a long and ineffectual search, fail to trace the animal. Salt comes to an end. More murmuring; and at last open mutiny. Consequently Domingo, the ringleader, another Spaniard, and the boy who came in with me are sent back to San Miguel.

Camp XIX.
April 8, 1867.

Ellen's birthday. Raining hard during night and in morning. I take my gun and rifle and wade and walk a good way up the creek and back before chocolate. Camp is broken up and sent on by Simon in two trips. Whilst waiting at the half-deserted camp, a fine tapir (called also Dante or mountain cow) strolled close up to me, and I was able to take a deliberate aim at the beast within 3 or 4 yards when the cap snapped. He still seemed undisturbed; when again drawing trigger, the rifle re-capped, another similar failure, and the discomfiture of seeing the Dante disappear at a lumbering trot. Our meat being short made it still more annoying. Simon and I then searched a dry creek with no success; and on returning, all stores are brought on and left in a small rancho till next Friday.

Halt. Camp XIX. to Letterbag Camp XX.
April 9, 1867.

Collinson and I proceed up a neighbouring dry creek in search of game; but are unsuccessful. Break up our camp, leaving stores in rancho, and move on a mile, where we are quickly followed by a relief-party under Eusebio, Julio, and Ezekiel, who bring in one horse, two oxen, and another left dying on the road. In meantime Perry, with the cutting-party, is badly wounded by a dry tree falling on him, and is carried back to camp, which we pitch in a convenient bend of the river. Hear of the death of Dr. Grand by cholera at Granada: sorry for his pretty widow.

Treefern Camp XXI.
April 10, 1867.

Stores sent for from Camp XIX. to Camp XX. Rearranging stores till after breakfast. Make up cartridges, build a rancho, and leave depôt of stores here. Eusebio, Julio, and Ezekiel, with Concepcion, return to San Miguel with letters from Collinson. Break up Camp XX., and move up to cutting-party; pass a pool, and when stooping to drink, find it guarded

by long black snake 10 feet long, which skedaddles quickly. Another small snake crossed in front of my feet the same afternoon. No game. Mosses in fantastic wreaths cover dead branches, making them even more lovely than when alive, if possible. Fern similar to large button-fern and magnificent specimens of *Coleoptera.* Camp at small stream under steep bank; make our quarters further than usual from main camp. Consultation overheard among the men as to the propriety of leaving us. Things begin to look bad.

Camp XXII. *Indian River?*
April 11, 1867.

Make up more cartridges before moving camp. Jaguars heard at night: however we do not think much of them. Magnificent tree-ferns with prickly stems (handsome section exhibited when cut). Walk alone to join party in front; pass through a lovely valley filled with birds of bright and lovely plumage. In one thicket, wherever the machetes had cut or scoured the bushes, a deep-red blood-like dye (*Anona reticulata*) or juice exuded (reminding one of Virgil, Bk. III.[*]) —Logwood, Fustic, Brazil-wood, and Nicaragua wood. In other places orange and purple dyes present similar exudations. St. Juan and Poro yield a beautiful yellow. Lichens abound; few fungi (too dry at present for them). Large branched tree-ferns covered with hairy knobs similar to stags' antlers. Firefly, when at rest, exhibits only two green lights, one on each side of its head, like a miniature steamer's starboard-light. When in motion, however, a reddish light from underneath is exhibited; and on flying through the air, the quicker the pace the brighter the abdominal light shines, sometimes scintillating and flashing, at other times steady, but always paling the two green signal-lights, which are insignificant in comparison. Each green light=light one English glowworm. The streams all flow the right way now, and we are no doubt in the water-basin of some system leading to the Atlantic, either Rama or Indian rivers. Delayed by a morass, across which Collinson throws a bridge; but most of the animals come to grief, refusing the bridge. No mosquitoes, and fewer ticks. Wonderfully brilliant fireflies and glow-worms; one of the latter similar to an illuminated pearl ring. Jaguars round the camp at night as usual.

To Observatory Camp, No. XXIII. *March.*
April 12, 1867.

Chiquot (Costa-Rican), when bringing in the oxen, finds tracks of tiger which had been prowling about them last night. For several days there have been some perplexing differences of reading between the compass-bearing and theodolite-angle; so we are anxious for a camp where we can observe the Pole-star or Southern Cross. The trees have been so impenetrable about us lately, that hitherto any view of the stars was impracticable. Easier ground fortunately for levelling and for the beasts of burden to pass, but difficult cutting through the bamboo-thicket. Cross a stream or two flowing to the north; this looks as if we were in the delta formed by the two branches of the Rama. The men kill a barber's-pole snake[†] and a curassow. Collinson put

---

[*] " Nam, quæ prima solo ruptis radicibus arbor
　　Vellitur, huic atro liquuntur sanguine guttæ,
　　Et terram tabo maculant."—*Æneid,* III. 27.

[†] This beautifully banded "barber's pole," or coral-snake (*Elaps*), whose bite is deadly, is marked as conspicuously as possible with bright bands of black, gold, and crimson; and so easily seen, known and avoided.

up a deer; but he was not armed, so unable to shoot it. In the course of the day I try the effect of leading the cutting-party with machete in hand. I plunge ahead; but find the effort too hard to keep up, and the heat too exhausting. Camp on N. side of stream flowing N.E., and clear it well, as we are to halt, as usual, two days. Deviation of compass, owing to small black grains of titanic iron in the lava and tuffs from this volcanic region, especially on sides of hill. Compass almost useless. This led probably to Cauty's result. At night we find we can see from our position both Pole-star and Southern Cross.

Halt. *Observatory Camp, No. XXIII.*

April 13, 1867.

Simon goes back with the mules for the bulk of provisions left at Camp No. XIX. I stay at camp all day making a rancho. One of the oxen breaks down, so is brought along without a load. The cutting-party are working slowly. The men discontented and provisions low. The cook Watson is most extravagant in his expenditure, and will not cook the beans, but expend at once flour and rice and such like economics. The men evidently contemplate deserting as soon as their time is up. Dine off rice and honey found in the woods, one small tin of potted meat, biscuit, and tea. We find the remaining small store of potted meat and liquor stolen so continually, that we lock up as a reserve store all remaining, and are to keep it for an emergency. I clear a spot from which in the evening we take some careful observations; and find the magnetic variation to be 4° 30′ East, at least 3 degrees different to what Mr. Collinson's calculations have been based on. Owing to the presence of unusual quantities of titanic iron, loose black grains of titaniferous sand with crystals of iserine (pseudomorphous) may be taken up by a magnet on shores of Lake Nicaragua in an unmixed state. Composition—oxide of iron with proportion of titanic acid or oxide of titanium; it is of no value in the arts, and presents the appearance of glittering coal-dust.

Halt at Observatory Camp, No. XXIII.

April 14, 1867.

Slight showers. Cool morning. A well-meaning curassow came close to the camp, and I was very happy to shoot him in time for dinner. According to the survey projected up to this time, we ought to be within nineteen miles of Rama Station, our destination. In the afternoon Collinson and I stroll out in the cutting and pass the curious open ground they cut through yesterday, with paths through the undergrowth of mountain cow, &c. Bring back a couple of guans; very acceptable to the camp, where meat is scarce.

March to Mutiny Rancho, Camp No. XXIV.

April 15, 1867.

Break up camp and move on, leaving proportion of stores in the rancho, with a note for any one who may follow us, directing them to it. Murmuring among the Caribs; their two months' engagement is up, they say, and they will not work any longer, so will start to-morrow morning. Meantime the cutting goes on as usual, and we make our camp on the north side of a small stream flowing S.E.

Halt at Mutiny Rancho, Camp No. XXIV.

April 16, 1867.

Many of the trees when cut or bruised give out poisonous juices ; and the scratches caused by thorns are very apt to fester &c. Our arms and legs suffer accordingly. Six of the Caribs (viz. *Gomes, Laurie, Pedro, Santo, Santiago,* and *Thomas*), with *Chiquot,* the tall Costa-Rican, desert in a body early this morning—stating, as their reason, that they could not live any longer on nothing but *frijolas,* which gave them, in their expressive language, "belly swell." Our party, although reduced to ten in all, resolve anyhow to reach the Atlantic. They are not allowed to take any provisions with them. Simon and I go back to last camp to guard and move up provisions for fear they should sack our stores. Shoot two guans. Our party now consists of 3 Englishmen, Collinson, Deering, and self; 2 Caribs, Perry and Simon ; 1 Creole (Jamaican), Watson ; 4 Spaniards (Nicaraguan), José, Bruno, Gregorio, Chiquot Perez. Do not move camp, but stay here. Make up cartridges and arrange stores, which are very small now. Go out with my gun after game, but return without success. The levelling will now have to be given up and just line chained and plotted. On returning from Observatory camp, I found a young chick guan, which I caught and kept alive. My hammock comes down with a run, and I have to spend the night on the ground, eaten alive by ticks *et hoc genus omne.*

Bedford Camp, No. XXV.

April 17, 1867.

Party now arranged as follows :—Collinson, with Simon, Perry, Gregorio, José, form cutting-party ; Deering chains with Bruno ; and I move the camp with Chiquot Perez. The pay of those men remaining with us is raised. The small kind of mosquito called strikers, which deposit a grub in your limbs, are very spiteful at No. XXIV. Camp. Break up camp. I shoot a cock curassow on the way ; and when we reach camp, find Collinson has shot a queen curassow, brown with white spots (*Crax fasciculata,* Crested Curassow), differently marked. On reaching a pretty stream, we breakfast, make our encampment. Soon after a party, consisting of Sonnernsten and Anderson with the Spaniard Domingo, reach us from San Miguelito. I get letters from home (announcing the birth of my second daughter, Katherine Rose) from Clara and my mother ; also one from Alice containing a page from 'Saturday Review' on my Madagascar book, and a journal from Willie. Morris had come into the cutting ; but an attack of fever compelled him to go back.

Halt at Bedford Camp, No. XXV.

April 18, 1867.

Sonnernsten leaves ; and I write a letter to Clara in answer to hers announcing the birth of my second daughter. This ought to leave by the American mail. Just as Sonnernsten is leaving, Capt. Pim arrives mounted on a good mule ; and having been only two days coming in, shows what can be done with good mules. Capt. Pim relates his serio-comic adventures up at the Javali mines. How Capt. Holman drew his revolver on him, and was accordingly shaken and summarily dismissed. Go on in the cutting with Capt. Pim and Collinson ; hit tributary of Rama River ; warm water, and no mistake about it. Named Susanna River in complement to Mrs. Pim. Capt.

Pim and self wade and walk a considerable way down the river. Get a nip of sherry and bitters, a great treat. Distance from San Miguelito 34 miles 870 yards. Level 398·62 feet above sea-level.

Halt at Bedford Camp, No. XXV.

April 19, 1867.

A Jamaica man named Collins, a muleteer, who Pim had engaged to bring the provisions into the cutting, arrived in the course of the morning. A holiday and cessation of work is also observed on account of Good Friday. Collins, it appears, on meeting the six Caribs who deserted us, allowed them to help themselves to whatever provisions they liked; and consequently the scrones were considerably lightened. For example, a sack of rice had diminished to 2 lbs., and others in proportion. A demijohn of rum containing 2½ gallons *leaked* or *evaporated* to as many pints. Mr. Dooring goes back to the last rancho with Ezekiel and Florentio, who stay in the cutting with Julio.

March to Easter-day Camp, No. XXVI.

April 20, 1867.

Pack up and leave Bedford Camp No. XXVII. Watson goes on to cook breakfast at the river. Breakfast delayed. Cutting crosses the river two or three times. After breakfast join the cutting-party, and cut the river again at Cecilia Falls. Shoot a macaw (green one) and a quail; and whilst waiting alone (on the spot I had selected to camp in) put a charge of B B into a Tigrillo or black mountain tiger-cat which came by hunting in a stealthy silent manner. Pass where Warree have been clearing all before them. Collins does not turn up till dark with the camp equipments.

Easter-day Camp, No. XXVI. Cecilia Falls.

April 21, 1867.

Rain during the night, so that there is a general drying when the sun comes out. Make the occasion a fête, in honour of which we eat a *pâté de foie gras*; and Watson, rather out in his dates, puts crosses on the flour dampers, and calls them hot cross buns. Bathe and swim in a fine pool below the falls. Look out for alligators, as the water is warm enough for them; and this stream, evidently a tributary to the Rama River, is called Susanna River; the falls are named with due ceremony, and after Mr. Collinson's wife Cecilia. A flag and staff is raised in a prominent position, and I secure a sketch of this charming spot. Serve out fish-hooks to all the men who wish for them; and we soon have plenty of fish for every one. Mountain mullet are first-rate eating. Observe the tiniest of humming-birds, one of the shady ones. One hardly knows which to admire most, the birds smaller than butterflies, or the butterflies larger than birds. One blue butterfly is a splendid fellow. The brilliant metallic-hued lizards are numerous; one has a curious yellow breathing-apparatus which projects from and retires to its breast. This lizard affects water. One with brilliant phosphoric blue tail; curious expansile throat: it is an anolis (*Anolis*). When frightened, it will often turn to bay and intimidate its foe by puffing out its throat. It frequents the banks and stones of these rivers.

March to River Camp, No. XXVII.

April 22, 1867.

Build a rancho, and leave behind us major portion of provisions which we are unable to carry, especially seven sacks of beans. The mule-train under Collins behave even worse than yesterday. Notice scarlet and blue tree-frogs, quite lively, which, however, exude a fœtid moisture which saves them from being preyed upon by snakes.

March to Sarsaparilla Camp, No. XXVIII., at Deering River.

April 23, 1867.

Collinson shoots a curassow, which is very acceptable. Collins leaves with most of his mules, and we keep two of them, which are certainly better than the others, but not so good as our own animals. Whilst Deering picks up the surveying behind, Collinson assists me in driving the mules, and they all, each and severally, come to especial grief in the bogs and ravines, of which we have to cross several. The bull turns out to be the best of the lot. Lose one mule in morass.

March to Quash Camp, No. XXIX.

April 24, 1867.

Leave camp by easy road after nearly losing one of the mules. Put up curassow from her nest, and miss a flying shot at her. Soon after, however, shoot a brace of chacalacas.

March to Javali Camp, No. XXX.

April 25, 1867.

Break up camp and move on. The country pretty easy but dry, and we breakfast on summit of high ridge, and eat the tree bare. The quequistas fail, and we make the most of our last taste of them. After putting the camp in motion, I go on with Collinson and the cutting-party. Through some bamboo-thicket I rouse up a deer, but, of course, not having bullets, a shot was out of the question. On the look out all day, but shoot nothing; plenty of macaws and parrots, but no game. In afternoon cross a dry watercourse; by hunting down it we find a pool about a quarter of a mile from the cutting, and I establish our camp in the watercourse. Catch a crab. Land-crab good size. This day passed wild vanilla; no pods upon the plant, however. Covered with garrapatas. There is no peace for the wicked.

March to Camp XXXI., Quequista Camp.

April 26, 1867.

Bruno came and aroused me early, with the intelligence that there were wild boar in the neighbourhood. I accompanied him down the stream, and soon find their tracks. Trace them through the woods, and come up with a large herd of them. I got a shot at one, and give him two barrels of BB, which have no effect on his tough hide. The whole herd bolt off sharp, and I pursue them some way, and, thinking Bruno was close behind me, did not take much notice of where I was going to; consequently, when I turned

round to retrace my steps, I found I had altogether missed my way, and had to wander about a long time before I reached camp. The cartridges are nearly all spoiled, so that it took four barrels to shoot a curassow. On arriving at stream saw two tapirs, and gave chase to one; got two shots with slug at one, but only wounded it. Camped here. Muddy stream, barely flowing; water bad; marshy banks. Men kill a long black water-snake. Pass the vines used by Indians for intoxicating fish.

Quequista Camp, No. XXXI.

April 27, 1867.

Simon sets out early to go back to the rancho at Cæcilia Falls for provisions, now reduced to tea, coffee, sugar, beans, native cheese. We have a few pots of potted meat in reserve. I go ahead with my gun and Collinson till breakfast time; Watson overtaking us with that meal at a small stream of good clear water. I shoot a guan before breakfast, at the foot of a steep hill we had surmounted. On the top of the hill we had passed a small cave, the earth of some wild beast or uncanny animal. Natives declare these caves, of which we saw more, to be made by owls. We all take quinine twice a day at present. Weather still dry in daytime, damp and chilly at night. Many small and elegant varieties of palms. My health lasts well, but continual perspiration and fatigue makes us all feel not quite up to the mark without any stimulant. Return to camp early. The cutting-party progress well, cutting the Susanna River again at 80°, which puts us in good spirits.

Halt at Quequista Camp, No. XXXI.

April 28, 1867.

Simon returns to camp, having brought up all the things but a small proportion of quequistas; apparently Collins had bagged the largest share of them on his way back. No good, however, to cry over spilt milk. One mule had come to grief in the same morass that we lost one in before—a veritable slough of despond. Collinson and I walk back to Javali Camp; see no game. Distance 39½ miles from San Miguelito, 251·27 feet above sea-level.

March to Dead-horse Camp, No. XXXII.

April 29, 1867.

By this time Charles the creolo and his party, with provisions, ought to be at Rama station, on the look out for us, and we are *at least* twelve miles from there, even according to Mr. Collinson's calculations; but, as far as I can make out, the localities have been so badly fixed, that we may be fifteen or twenty miles off. As there is no game to be shot, we are expending the potted meat daily. Walk up as far as the river, which we cross, Collinson leaving a note in a prominent position, to be seen by any one ascending the stream. Breakfast across the river, which now is a really important stream. I descend alone two or three bends of the river, as far as its junction with Deering River; below, the river seems deep and navigable for large canoes, which gives hope that we may be nearer than we imagine. This day we only have four animals to carry the camp &c. Horse very weak, lies down continually; and one mule has a lump on its side suspiciously like a broken rib; and from the amount of tumbling and rolling it has had, it is only what

could be expected. No game to be seen or shot. Make our camp late at the extremity of cutting. Mr. Deering has another attack of fever. Troubled with mosquitoes. Species of insect with wings like two dead leaves.

Frijolas Camp, No. XXXIII.

April 30, 1867.

Up early and hunting unsuccessfully for game. Hear a curassow, but cannot get near him. The bird makes a peculiar booming noise, but it is of a kind that it is difficult to know from what direction it comes. The horse gives up its life, poor beast. El Toro and El Macho hold out the best. Whilst packing up the camp, Chiquot marks a curassow, which I shoot. G. D. Break up camp and join cutting-party; Mr. Deering coming up in time for breakfast together in a hot open bit. Cutting-party work well. Simon hears some curassow, and I leave the track and hunt after them, and get a brace, a fine cock and hen. Camp in a nice open-wooded valley, good water. Catch a land-tortoise with an enormous garrapata on it.

March to North Rama Camp, No. XXXIV.

May 1, 1867.

Plenty of Gamalote long grass on banks. The beasts wander far, and are difficult to find; at last the small macho is found, but the bull is lost, so now two beasts only remain, and one is not worth much. Breakfast off curassow and frijolas; join the cutting-party when they hit the main branch of North Rama River, which we cross, making our camp on further side. See an alligator for the first time since we left the lake. Perry declares that he recognizes the river, and says that we are about ten miles from Rama station; but eventually confesses that it is only conjecture on his part. None of the Caribs are ever to be believed. Traces of Dantes at water's edge, and other large game. Fish caught by Ezekiel. Large eboe-trees, and, consequently, coxendeer, a large species of black ant, with malicious nippers in its large head. Towards early morning, before daylight, the dew is condensed on the summits of the lofty trees and drips down—the changes of temperature up aloft being greater, whilst under their shelter the temperature is more agreeable. It is difficult to estimate the height of trees. Collinson puts the limit at 300 feet, and he is experienced. I put it at a lower figure. Camp on north side of Rama. I proceed a short way further with Collinson. See plenty of iguanas; plenty of garrapatas, and mosquitoes increase in numbers and activity.

Halt, North Rama Camp, No. XXXIV.

May 2, 1867.

This morning the stores are examined, and only one day's supply of frijolas remaining. Simon goes back with José and Perez to the rancho, at No. XXXI. camp, and, consequently, we have to halt to-day instead of Saturday. Shoot a guan marked by Mr. Deering's party, when we overtake them. Collinson and self go on to cutting-party, and reach them where the cutting crosses a little stream; ascend it a short way to cross it without getting very wet, and select a good spot, where we breakfast. After breakfast heavy thunder showers come down, and I, after hunting in front of the cutting till 2.30, set out alone to go back to camp. Before reaching place

where we had breakfasted, met Deering and levelling-party; pass them, and whilst creeping under a steep bank in a gully, on reaching level ground hear something spring, and, turning, see a puma who I am forced to shoot in the head. He tumbles into the stream. I fetch Deering and one of his men, who assist me in dragging out the beast and skinning him. On my way home I meet wild boars, but fail to get a shot. Simon returns without the cargo-bull, which is a great loss.

Halt, North Rama Camp, No. XXXV.

May 3, 1867.

Collinson leaves with Perry, Julio, José, Chopin, and Ezekiel, with small mule and provisions for two days, to cut to the fork of the Rama River. We meantime, viz. Deering, Simon, Watson, Florentio, Chiquot, Perez, remain at camp. Prepare a raft to float down the party and provisions. Raft is composed of ten planks of mountain mohoe, split—a light wood, something similar to the trumpet tree, floats like cork; a small platform is arranged in the centre, on which the provisions (now much reduced) are stored, and is christened the "Mountain Cow." At night at 8.30 we hear the distant report of Collinson's gun, and fire a rocket in reply. Florentio brought in a brace of guans, which was satisfactory.

No. XXXIV. Camp to No. XXXV. Camp, both on Rama River.

May 4, 1867.

Embark tents, provisions, &c., and proceed round the point, where I shoot a brace of guans and catch a fine guapote for breakfast. After the monotonous tramping through the woods, the movement of the raft is delightful. The raft is composed of nine split halves of mountain mohoe timber, fastened by two polancas crosswise, and bound with withes or behookas. Ezekiel arrives with a letter from Collinson, upon which we break up our station, and, after breakfast, float down the calm still waters of the Rama, along still lake-like reaches. Sun very hot; we have been so accustomed to the shade of the forest, that we feel it very much on our heads. We arrived at the falls about 2 P.M., and at once set to work to take the raft to pieces, floating it piecemeal over the falls, and preparing it ready for next day. Construct tent &c. among the trees some way from the bank. Disturbed by wild beasts at night.

Start on raft down the River Rama.

May 5, 1867.

At first we glided down the river calmly enough, the men pushing our raft along with their "polancas;" but after about a couple of hours we came on rocks and rapids, over which the raft could not be passed, but had to be taken laboriously to pieces, and pulled over stick by stick. While this operation was being performed we saw a jaguar of an extraordinary size, fully as large as a Bengal tiger, cross a small tributary running into the river on the right, and make towards us. The raft was fortunately ready for embarkation again; so we deprived our friend—who, I believe, would have attacked the whole party—of the chance of a meal. I must here note that, like all else, our bullets had long since been expended, and it would have been foolhardiness to court a contest with such a brute against BB shot.

During this day no less than five rapids were passed; and so laborious was the work of taking to pieces and putting together the raft, that we travelled scarcely more than two miles. The river was a succession of long pools, 15 to 20 feet deep, and about 150 feet wide, with scarcely a perceptible current, connected sometimes by rapids, with gravelly bottom strewed with boulders, and at others by crevasses in the basaltic rocks, in which the water would be confined in narrow, tortuous, and grimly black passages, down which it rushed boiling and frothing to another silent pool.

A few banana-trees were seen before night, which gave us hopes that we might fall in with Indians. In times passed some of the Ramas must have come up as far as this point. There were plenty of water-fowl, bittern and cinereous boatbills (*Cancroma cochlearii*), with their queer beaks.

At the head of one of these romantic chasms we camped the first night. The wild animals always use these contractions of the river for crossings, as they can jump from one rock to the other without entering the water. So many jaguars and tapirs, who have a peculiar penchant for trampling out fires, surrounded us during the night, that we had to keep watch turn by turn for fear of an attack, while those not on duty, having left their hammocks behind, would seek the most comfortable holes in the rocks and curl themselves up to sleep until their turn for watching arrived.

Second Day's Voyage on Raft down the Rama River.

May 6, 1867.

We are up betimes, and whilst the men are hauling the logs of the raft over the rocky barrier, which here dams the river, into the pool beneath, I find a few remaining fish-hooks in an envelope (a last present from my brother Farquharson), and catch some *savallo* and guapote, of which we make a good breakfast, *i. e.* about 4 lbs. of fish to us six men. We embark again on our frail craft, and, after continual windings and many turns of the river, whose banks are now further apart, we halt for a midday meal. The water-fowl are numerous, including various herons (*Ardea virescens*, *A. candidissima*, *A. cærulea*), Alcedininæ, as *Ceryle torquata*, *C. cabanisi*, *C. amazonia*, as well as the fish-eating toucan (*Ramphastos piscivorus*), and rails (*Aramides* and *Porzana*, sp.?). More rapids and longer stretches of open water, over the deeper parts of which we float with the stream lazily, and using the polancas when shallow enough. Before evening I bagged two large, fat, female iguanas as well as a bittern (*Tigrisoma?*). Arriving at some falls before night, we halt and bivouac for the night.

May 7, 1867.

Early this morning fishing, and find a nest of alligator's eggs in the sand; open some of them and find the young alligators nearly hatched, and quite alive and lively try them as bait for "guapote," but they do not answer well. Still rapids and pools alternately presented themselves, and so frequently came the former, that more than three-quarters of the day we were up to our waists in water, passing our "mountain mahoe" logs down the torrents. Halted at a lovely spot to breakfast on a large iguana I shot, and where the butterflies were noticeable for their beauty, as *Urania sloaneus*, *U. leilus*, &c. Resuming our voyage, we floated down a long beautiful stretch of the tranquil waters of the Rama. On a sudden, turning a sharp corner, a cheer burst from all hands; for there ahead of us, not 300 yards distant, on a prominent rock jutting out into the river, was Captain Pim, accom-

panied by Charles (the "Boss" of Collinson's 1863 expedition) and another Creole, who represented our provisioning party. The Atlantic and Pacific were at last united, and all our anxieties were at rest.

After the first joy of meeting had subsided, on inquiry we found that the bulk of our provisions had been left outside the bar of the Rama, in a sheltered nook called Grindstone Bay, as the sea was running too high at the time to admit of a safe entrance for a loaded canoe.

Collecting together all the party had brought up with them, we sent some men back to Mr. Deering to inform him of our success and stay his further progress down the river.

We then continued the descent of the river, and, following the party to where their canoes had been left, we came on the grandest falls yet seen. We had often heard rumours from the natives of the "Big Falls" just above the junction of the north and south branches, and of their terrible nature, but until then had set down much to their fondness for exaggeration. But we were rapidly undeceived, and understood how easily the superstitious feelings of the Indians would be worked on by the sight that now met my eyes. The river running its placid course between low banks covered with "scutch"-grass, wild plantains, tree-ferns, and the venerable spreading Indian fig-tree, clothed with a matting of creepers (*Bauhinias*), and vines falling down over the water from their overhanging branches, like a curtain, suddenly changed: a great upheaval of volcanic rock, which had evidently, by damming the river, formed the long deep pool above, barred its progress, but opened a narrow winding passage, down which the water rushed for over half a mile, and dashing up against the caverns it had hollowed underneath, often obstructed in its course by immense masses of rock hurled by some convulsions of nature into the stream, sent for miles an ominous sound like confined thunder. The rocks, bare of vegetation, and frowning up black and perpendicular from the waters, completed the weird contrast of the picture.

Bivouac below falls, Rama River. To mouth of river. Canoe.

May 8, 1867.

This day, the 8th, we arrived at Rama Station, an old Indian village. We then continued our voyage as far as the first inhabited Indian village. The chief, who had assumed the name of "Shepherd," soon recognized us and held out the right hand of fellowship. This man is about the finest Indian I ever met—a Rama, though perhaps hardly pure, as he has a slight moustache, but preserving all the other characteristics, clean shining brown skin, height fully 6 feet (though, from his immense breadth and muscular power, he seemed much shorter), with an intelligent expression and severe and determined countenance. He soon stirred up his wife, who, according to their rigid laws, may not speak to any one out of the tribe, and ordered her to prepare some "mishla" for us, but, at my request, without the chewing process. This *mishla* is a drink prepared in a similar manner to the "kava" of the South Sea Islands, out of cassada (*Jatropha manihot*), ripe plantains, pine-apples, and cocoa-nuts.

Indian village. Mouth of River Rama to Greytown. By sea in canoe.

May 9, 1867.

At 3 A.M., in a heavy shower of rain, sleeping like a babo, but perfectly

E

wet through, I am awakened by Capt. Pim, who tells me that we have arrived at the village at the mouth of the Rama River. We soon take up our quarters in an empty hut, and renew our damp slumbers, in our still dripping rugs, till 6 A.M., when a cup of rye coffee and a ripe banana, followed by a hasty bathe, revived us; and after hastily swallowing a cup of coffee, we started off for the bar, knowing the necessity of crossing it as soon as possible, for fear of one of the gales which often occur at that season of the year arising and stopping our progress. To our intense disappointment the bar was declared impracticable, there being three distinct lines of breakers, one outside the other; two were the limit, our men said, they could cross in safety; nevertheless we determined to cross.

Tincum's village, a collection of about twenty huts, was certainly a model Indian settlement; the huts were all beautifully built of stout posts of lancewood (*Duguetia quitarensis*), filled in with the tough "sillico" stems, and roofed with the leaves of the swamp-growing "scumfm." They were incomparably superior to the wretched Spanish hovels of San Miguelito, and showed strongly the superiority of the pure Indian over the mongrel descendants of his race and the Spanish conquerors. The hatred of the Ramas for the Spaniards was intense, and only the friendly feeling of the former towards me saved the latter from destruction. Before parting Shepherd gave the Spaniards a hint that if they ever came to his country alone, he would have the greatest pleasure in killing them all. The statement was made in such a serious matter-of-fact way that I could not help laughing; but the poor Spaniards, gazing on the giant's proportions, evidently did not feel safe or happy until they had left him some way behind.

In spite of our men's warning of the still dangerous appearance of the bar, our patience was exhausted, and we determined to try it; packing our canoes we steered steadily for it, and, watching our opportunity, darted over with a slight ducking, but in perfect safety. That evening we slept at "Great Grindstone Bay," as the men feared the Greytown bar at night. Sandflies innumerable bit us during our hasty sleep. At 11 P.M. we re-embarked, had plenty of rain, and arrived at Greytown over a tranquil bar at half-past 8 next morning. So ragged and wet and worn, without shoes or stockings, which had long since quitted us, were we on arriving, that the honest people hardly knew us; but a good sleep, wash, and decent clothes soon put us to rights. Our health, notwithstanding all hardships, had never been better.

Greytown.

May 10, 1867.

Pim embarked in the 'Santiago de Cuba' steamer, in which (on his way to New York) he was wrecked a few days subsequently on the coast of New Jersey, five lives being lost in the attempt to land. As I now remained a few days at Greytown, it may be as well to describe it.

Greytown and adjacent country.

May 11, 1867.

Greytown is important as the only port possessed by Nicaragua on its Atlantic coast, and is situated in 11° N. lat. and 84° W. long. The place itself is insignificant enough, as a glance at the accompanying view of the interior of the harbour will show; at the same time it is of strategical importance in many ways, and its history is not uninteresting. The climate is

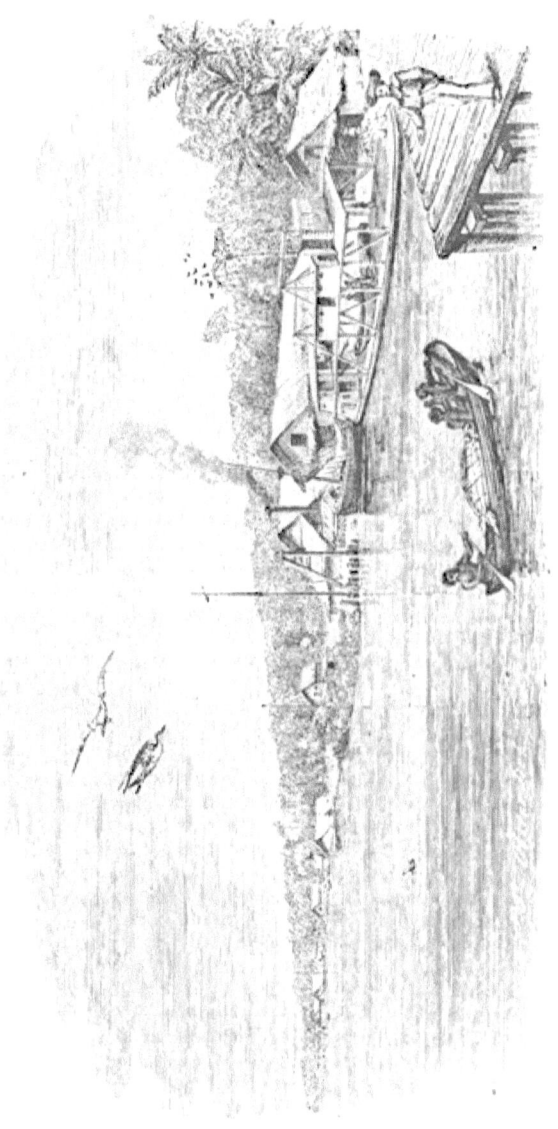

humid, and along the low coast-lands a tropical heat prevails. The heat is never oppressive while the trade-winds blow, but during calms it is sultry and overpowering. The prevailing type of disease appears to be a low form of intermittent fever, which is not to be wondered at, considering that Greytown is built upon a swamp. June, July, and August are considered the unhealthy months, and January, February, and March the healthiest; the thermometer seldom exceeds 82° Fahr., or falls below 71° Fahr. in the shade.

SEASONS.

RAINY.	DRY.
June.	January.
July.	February.
⅔ August.	March.
⅓ October.	April.
November.	May.
December.	⅓ August.
	⅔ October.
The rain descends in a perfect deluge, accompanied by thunder and lightning.	Sometimes not a drop of rain falls, but generally it is showery, even in the so-called dry season at Greytown.

In the interior, where the forest vegetation has been cleared away in the neighbourhood of the islands and lakes, the seasons are more marked, and the dry season is really dry, not a drop falling. At times Greytown is visited by terrible gales or hurricanes, styled "Northers;" at such times the trade-wind is gradually killed, and a calm precedes the coming storm, the barometer falls rapidly, and the clouds bank up in the horizon. After these warnings the norther commences without further prelude, and in an incredibly short time the sea is churned up into great and violent waves, whilst the surf on the bar is terrific. A norther will sometimes last for three whole days.

The whole civilized population of the Nicaraguan and neighbouring republics is collected on the Pacific side of Central America, the Caribbean coasts being almost entirely uninhabited, with the exception of a few independent tribes of Indians along the banks of the large rivers, like the Indian and Rama. The principal tribes are the Valiente, Rama Cookwra, Woolwa Tonga, and Poya tribes, all interesting from an ethnological point of view, especially as they are fast disappearing. There is generally a small camp of some of these tribes on the sandy spit (Punta d'Arenas) at the entrance to Greytown harbour, who catch and sell turtle &c. Accounts of these Mosquito tribes will be found in the 'Journal of the Royal Geographical Society,' 1862, p. 242, &c., by Mr. Bell, and in the last volume of 'Memoirs of the Anthropological Society,' by Mr. Collinson. This region, *i.e.* the valley and lowlands of the San Juan and the lakes of Nicaragua and Managua, is more particularly interesting to naturalists and geologists, as forming the borderland between two of the great primary distributional provinces for the terrestrial vertebrata in the present world recognized by Professor Huxley, viz., the boundary line betwixt *Austro-Columbia* and *Arctogæa*; for it was in this direction apparently that, during the Miocene epoch, these two great land divisions were separated by that great equinoctial ocean whose currents rolled from eastward beyond and over the present sites of the Sahara deserts and the plains of Hindostan.

As the line of the American Cordilleras was upheaved, the continents more nearly approached each other, an archipelago of detached volcanic summits probably first indicating the future isthmus, whilst the bounds of the ocean were narrowed, and, previous to the actual junction, but a narrow channel or strait was left. It is supposed that the last indication of this strait is yet observable in the line of the San Juan and the waters drained by it. This theory has received substantial support from the observations of Mr. Osbert Salvin, the well-known ornithologist, who, from long studying the peculiarities of the Central-American bird-fauna, has come to the conclusion that an oceanic separation is plainly indicated as having formerly existed between Costa Rica and the country north of the Nicaraguan lakes. This upheaval has by no means ceased, and the lakes of Managua and Nicaragua, up to which the Spanish galleons proceeded *viâ* the San Juan, are now 156 and 128 feet respectively above the mean level of the two oceans, so that now with difficulty stern-wheel light-draught steamers, drawing but 18 inches of water, make their way between the rapids, their cargo having to be shifted across these impediments. A rise of 6 feet in the waters of the lakes enables bongos to pass the rapids in the wet season.

Every year apparently adds to the difficulties of the navigation, which Mr. Collinson attributes to the continual rise of the Pacific coast. Indeed it is not improbable, if a careful series of observations were established, that after a lapse of years the rate of rise might be ascertained, which, if compared with seismological observations in the same district, would prove of the utmost value and interest.

It has been before noticed that Greytown is the only settlement of any size on the Caribbean coast, owing to its position at the mouth of the San Juan river, which is the only one which offers facilities for transit across the isthmus; and consequently a portion of the Californian traffic has for some years passed in this channel, an enterprising American company having monopolized the "transit route." Owing, however, to the rapid silting-up of the embouchure of the San Juan at Greytown, this town would infallibly have lost all its importance, had it not been that the rapid development of marine telegraphy has given rise to a great demand for India-rubber, a valuable kind of which is collected from trees which are numerous in the dense forests of the Central-American isthmus, especially on the Atlantic coast.

Greytown is the principal port for the export of india-rubber on the coast. It is collected by parties of Indians, Caribs, or half-caste creoles, seldom by Europeans, to whom the dealers (who are also storekeepers) advance the necessary outfit of food, clothing, and apparatus for collecting rubber, on condition of receiving the whole of the rubber collected at a certain rate. The rubber-hunters are termed *Uleros* (*Ule* being the Creole term for rubber). A party of Uleros, after a final debauch at Greytown, having expended all their remaining cash, generally make a start in a canoe for one of the rivers or streams which abound on the coast, and, having fixed on a convenient spot for a camp, commence operations. The experienced rubber-hunter marks out all the trees in the neighbourhood. The rubber-tree is the *Castilloa elastica*, which grows to a great size, being on an average about 4 feet in diameter, and from 20 to 30 feet to the first spring of the branches. From all the trees in the almost impenetrable jungle hang numerous trailing parasites, lianes, &c.; from these, and especially the tough vines, are made rude ladders, which are suspended close to the trunks of the trees selected, which are now slashed by machetes in diagonal cuts from right to left, so as to meet

in the middle in central channels, which lead into iron gutters driven in below, and these again into the wooden pails. The pails are soon full of the white milk, and are emptied into larger tin pans. The milk is next pressed through a sieve, and subsequently coagulated by a judicious application of the juice of a Bejuca (an *Apocyna?*) vine. The coagulated mass is then pressed by hand, and finally rolled out on a board with a wooden roller. The rubber has now assumed the form of a large pancake, nearly two feet in diameter and about a quarter of an inch thick, on account of which they are termed *tortillas* by the Uleros; these cakes are hung over the side poles and framework which supports the *rancho*, which is erected in the woods, and allowed to dry for about a fortnight, when they are ready to be packed for delivery to the dealer.

In the meantime others of the party go in pursuit of game, such as tapirs or *dantas*, or mountain cows as they are termed, of which there are several species; or they harpoon the manatee*, which they dexterously follow in their canoes, as it cannot remain under water long. The point of the harpoon used by the Indians is movable, and, attached to a line and floating reel, it becomes detached from the shaft when the siren is struck. The wild boar or javali (domestic pig run wild?) and the *waree*, or peccary, which are shot in June or July, and the deer, which are shot in December, afford good pork and venison. The waters of all the numerous rivers and lakes are characterized by an astounding number of distinct ichthyological faunæ. The Indians are good fishermen, and will shoot fish in the water by bow and arrow, or cut them down with a machete; the best fish are perhaps the *guapote*, *mojarra*, and *savallo*. By way of feathered game the curassows and guans (*Crax alector*, *C. fasciolata*, and several penelopes) of different species are of good size and flavour; whilst iguanas and land-turtle eggs serve to vary the bill of fare of the Ulero gourmet.

The picnic life of the Ulero is not all *couleur de rose*. At night the jaguar and pumas (*Felis onca*, *F. melas*, and *F. concolor*) will prowl in the neighbourhood of the *rancho*. These beasts are sometimes brought to bay with dogs by the Carib mahogany cutters in the fork of a low tree and then speared; the spear in this instance is always provided with a stout cross bar, to prevent the transfixed animal from reaching his assailant.

Besides this the alligators abound in the water, which renders bathing slightly precarious; but, as a general rule, these brutes are cowardly enough when not hungry. On one occasion one of the party (with whom the author was in these woods) having shot a dante, which sank to the bottom of the river Rama, an Indian dived after it to attach a rope to the carcase, while the alligators, attracted by the smell of blood, surrounded the canoe in a circle of some score yards in diameter, but none of them ventured an attack on the bold diver. Both Caribs and Indians have a profound contempt for the alligators in these rivers. On shore, again, the snakes are numerous, such as the *taboba*, *vipera de sangre*, a long black snake, *Coryphodon constrictor*, the lovely coral and barber-pole snakes, and, worst of all, the small

---

* The genus *Manatus* appears to be the most ubiquitous of the suborder Sirenia, and various species are to be found, not only on the rivers, inland lakes, and coasts of Tropical America, but along the entire opposite coast of Africa, where the habitat of the *Manatus senegalensis* extends round the Cape and as far north on the Mozambique coast as the river Zambesi; besides which its presence is recorded in the lake Shirwa by Dr. Kirk. A species, *M. vogelii*, also occurs in the Upper Niger, and, according to Barth, in lake Tsad; whilst Heuglin notices one species in the Tana Sea in Abyssinia. So it is not improbable that the *Manatus* may occasionally meet its East-Indian congener the *Halicore dugong*.

tamagusa or "tommygoff." The Caribs assert the valuable properties of a vine (a species of *Aristolochia*) which they declare will allay the effects of a snake-bite.

The greatest drawbacks, however, to the enjoyment of Ulcro life in Mosquitia and Costa Rica are the swarms of garrapatas or ticks (*Ixodes*), which persecute remorselessly the hunter or woodsman. The *chijoe* or jigger is also another annoyance. By-the-bye, it is said, I do not know on what grounds, that this last-mentioned pest is only to be found where domestic swine are kept. I only know that I have suffered from one in the woods many miles from any domesticated swine. Do they appear, therefore, where there are wild hog or peccary? There is also a disgusting bot-fly and swarms of mosquitoes near the water.

The Formicidæ are likewise numerous and formidable; a gigantic black ant, which especially pervaded the oboe (*Dipterix oleifera*) trees, is justly dreaded, and we always avoided slinging our hammocks from these trees if possible. Stout Indians will howl and writhe with agony from the effect of their bites. A minute red fire ant also infests the acacia trees, and is barely more endurable. The howling of the black monkeys also is not conducive to sleep when they choose some neighbouring branches for their "serenade." The above slight sketch may serve to give some insight into the pleasure of a country life in the vicinity of Greytown; pleasures, however, of which the Nicaraguan citizens seldom avail themselves.

There have already appeared in 'Nature' some accounts of peculiar nocturnal vibrations observable in iron vessels off Greytown, which I will not allude to further.

The drawing which accompanies this notice was taken from the pier of the Transit Company's wharf; the town itself is barely visible from this point, and lies beyond the few buildings shown. The remains of one of the flat-bottomed steamers which ascend the river is shown lying by the shore. Canon Kingsley appears to have been disappointed at only twice catching a glimpse of the back-fin of a shark during his recent visit to the West Indies; let me recommend the bar of Greytown Harbour and its vicinity as an exceptionally favourable locality for studying these monsters in their native element.

Greytown. Steamer 'Danube.'
May 12, 1867.

The English mail steam-packet arrives, and, after some three hours' delay at Mr. Paton's, we obtain our letters at Hollenbeck's. I receive good news from home, with exception of dear Willie's severe attack of illness at Plymouth; also that my people have taken Eastern Villa, at Anglesey. In afternoon hire a canoe and go out to the steamer, which turns out to be my old friend the 'Danube.' Accordingly I go on board with Morris, who pays $1·75 for canoe, and we remain to dinner at Capt. Rooks's invitation, and stay to sleep on board. Every thing seems so English and clean after the filth we have been accustomed to. When I first reached the steamer, my appearance was thin, haggard, and badly dressed. I was not recognized, and I was obliged to tell the Captain who I was, and at last they remembered who I was. Nothing can exceed the kindness and civility of the Captain and officers, and I, of course, had some long yarns to spin about my sojourn in the interior. The temptation to go to England, now that I am on board an English steamer, is very hard; and, if I am troubled with more vexations on shore, I shall decidedly go off with the 'Danube.'

"On embarking on board the *Danube* steamer, lying at anchor in the road-stead off Greytown on the 12th May, 1867, I was informed that the ship was haunted by most curious noises at night since she had arrived, and that the superstitious black sailors were much frightened at what they thought must be a ghost.   The captain and officers could make nothing of it, and it afforded a great matter for discussion.   On inquiry I found out that other *iron* ships had been similarly affected.   Curiously enough this noise was only heard at night, and at certain hours.   Some attributed it to fish, suckers, turtle, &c., others to the change of tide or current; but no satisfactory conclusion could be arrived at.   When night came on there was no mistake about the noise; it was quite loud enough to awaken me, and could be heard distinctly all over the ship.   It was not dissimilar to the high monotone of an Æolian harp, and the noise was evidently caused by the vibration of the plates of the iron hull, which could be sensibly perceived to vibrate.   What caused this peculiar vibration ?   Not the change of current and tide, because, if so, it would be heard by day.   Like every thing else that we cannot explain, I suppose we must put it down to electricity, magnetism, &c.   If this should meet the eye of any of the officers of the above-mentioned steamer, or others who have noticed this phenomenon, I should be glad to hear whether this effect still continues, or if any satisfactory conclusion has yet been arrived at.   I may add that from the hold of the vessel the grunts of the toad-fish could be distinctly heard."

'*Danube.*'   *Greytown.*   *On Shore.*
May 13, 1867.

Sea beautifully calm ; but hot sun.   Lighters alongside taking off cargo. After breakfast, about 10.30 A.M., I go on shore with Morris on one of these lighters.   The waves hardly break on the bar ; and a shark or two are visibly cruising with their back-fin showing above the water, a ripple behind them attending their passage through the water.   There are so many sharks here, and they are so voracious, that if a boat does swamp here, long before any swimmer could reach the sand bank, he would be torn in pieces by these fish, which will follow men into water not over their knees.   Sharks and alligators are horrid-looking objects; and I do not know which are the worst; but the former are bolder, and certainly more to be feared.   Decide to go to England by this mail.   No signs of Griffiths, who ought to be back from the Colorado by this time.

Greytown.   *San Juan del Norte.*
May 14, 1867.

Griffiths arrives last night without any thing.   Spend my time in writing a long letter to Collinson and in packing up the things asked for at Rama River.   The men under Francis refuse to start in the canoe for the Rama River, as the wind is not right, they say.   Francis expresses his ability of going that afternoon ; but when time comes he disappears.   In the mean-time all these men are earning 1¼ dollar apiece per diem.   Walk with Morris along the bank of the river.   See a man with land-turtle,which, he says, are plentiful, and come up at this time of year to lay their eggs on the shore.

Greytown.   *San Juan del Norte.*
May 15, 1867.

I got on board the '*Danube*' steamer with Morris and the miner and all our traps, and, with no feelings of regret, said good-bye to the inhospitable hores of Nicaragua.   Francis started for Rama River at 10 A.M.

Off Greytown. '*Danube*' *put to sea.*

May 16, 1867.

This morning felt freer and happier than I had done for some time past. I now begin to realize that I am actually on my way home, and already count the days when I shall see little Kate. A gun is fired at 10 A.M. to warn the P. O. authorities; and about noon, after a few turns of the paddles to our anchor, the mails are taken on board, and we really get off. Till we were really steaming away, I felt I might at any moment be recalled to shore, and was not perfectly at ease until the shore slowly faded and Torlingas Hill sank in distance. Slight attack of fever; take pill and turn in early.

At sea. '*Danube.*' *Aspinwall.*

May 17, 1867.

Take Seidlitz powder in the morning; very feverish all day long. Hot, but nice breeze all day. Ship seems very empty. Only passengers besides self and Morris are Jacobi, a German Jew, who has made money in Greytown, and a Jesuit priest of unprepossessing exterior. We sight land soon after noon, and reach Aspinwall about 5 P.M. Warping alongside wharf, narrowly escaping fouling with Liverpool steamer 'Columbian.' Go on shore with Morris, who seems a good-natured fellow enough, and buy some books to read. Yellow fever at Aspinwall; wonderful how, indeed, the town of Colon has escaped depopulation. Vessels from St. Thomas bearing and landing their dead and dying of the pest. No sanitary regulations. Inhabitants tried to build shed-huts to put the sick into. Panama and Taboga suffer also severely, the fever at Taboga being brought by through-passengers and baggage from W. Indies and Colon.

Alongside Wharf. Aspinwall. '*Danube*' *Steamer.*

May 18, 1867.

Very hot and close all day. Thermometer about 84° Fahr. Showery at intervals. Went on shore with the Admiralty Agent and Morris, and got my hair cut at a nigger's establishment: charged 50 cents. The scent which he rubbed on my head as a finish had a villainous odour of bad rum and water. Reading and writing, lounging; too hot to do any thing except in the way of iced Seltzer. The 'Columbian' (Liverpool steamer) rapidly filling up with cargo at adjacent wharf. So hot down below that I try sleeping on deck till 1 A.M.

Alongside Wharf. Aspinwall. '*Danube*' *Steamer.*

May 19, 1867.

The Pacific Steam Company's vessel 'Henry Chauncey' arrived from New York with nine hundred and odd passengers, including three hundred Federal troops. These were all despatched in two or three trains the same morning to Panama. Dr. Totten (son of Col. Totten?), the Surgeon of the 'Henry Chauncey,' comes on board 'Danube.' We go on shore and get latest news from Europe, May 11th, by telegraph. In afternoon Morris and self go on shore and walk on coral reef. Admire natural aquarium on it; wonderful long spined *Echidni*, &c. Then walk along the borders of the mangrove-swamp and back by a road to the town. Aspinwall is a filthy dirty hole; and to-day heat and mosquitoes and flies render it intolerable.

Alongside Wharf. Aspinwall. 'Danube.'

May 20, 1867.

Very slow work waiting at Aspinwall so many days. If I had money I would break the time by visiting Panama; but Capt. Reeks is kind enough to ask Mr. Martin about a bill for me. I go to Mr. Martin's office, who instructs me to go to Mr. Field's, where I inquire if they will buy a bill, and learn that after a couple of hours I shall know. And I then visit Mr. Parker, the Superintendent of the Panama Railway Company, and obtain from him two complimentary tickets for self and Morris to Panama and back. Talk with him about the Nicaragua line, &c. Walk with Morris along the railway-line. Mr. Field, who is going to England in this boat, declined to cash my bill; so that I shall probably be unable to visit Panama. Mr. Parker subsequently shot dead in his office by a ruffian with a revolver for not giving him a ticket.

Alongside Aspinwall Wharf. 'Danube.'

May 21, 1867.

Walk on shore by the pier and church, and eat some mangoes with Mr. Morris. Meet Mr. Parker, the Superintendent of the Panama line. Dull and sultry morning. Coaling by after-gangway. About noon the Royal Mail-steamer 'Tyne' arrives, by which we get files of papers up to May 2, and by the 'Henry Chauncey' we got telegraphs up to May 11; so now we are not so very much behind the world.

Alongside Wharf. 'Danube' Steamer. Aspinwall.

May 22, 1867.

It rained during the night as if the very heavens were melting. Hotter than ever. Writing up journal and reading or pacing the deck fills up in some way the time, which hangs heavy enough on our hands. Dull rainy morning with hot sun in afternoon. Avocada or alligator-pears are now in season, and we have them served at each meal; they are best eaten and considered as a vegetable. Our amusement consists in watching the niggers engaged in placing the wrought-iron screw-piles, of which the wharf is being built. Most of the passengers on the 'Tyne' are for New Zealand. This day the Jesuit priest left this ship and proceeded on board the 'Tyne,' *en route* for Carthagena.

Alongside Wharf. 'Danube.' Aspinwall.

May 23, 1867.

This morning thermometer is 87° in the companion. Very hot. Stories of the Doctor's adventures last night; he is unable to appear at breakfast. Leave my cabin aft in saloon and change to one on the main-deck forward to make room for passengers expected to-day. Roasting hot. Engineer's store-keeper tumbles down the hatchway and fractures his skull. Not so bad as expected. At 3.30 P.M. leave Aspinwall, not waiting for the North Pacific mails and specie, which is late. The Admiralty agent, however, insists on the vessel leaving; and we are all glad to get to sea. Heavy showers and squalls. There are several passengers: ex-Bishop of Lima, late Chargé d'Affaires also from Lima, two Browns, one rich and the other poor.

Alongside Wharf. 'Danube.' At sea.

May 24, 1867.

Hotter than ever. Passengers arranging themselves on board. Put to sea at 3.30 P.M.; as the N. Pacific mail-boat had not been signalled, we could wait no longer for her. Spend most of my time on main-deck forward, where it is cooler. Blacks flying about. Wind dead ahead.

At sea. 'Danube.'

May 25, 1867.

No water available for bath. After breakfast play backgammon with Naval agent till luncheon. Read Hampshire newspaper with account of ball at Newtown? *Bal costumé.* Dresses mentioned of Mrs. L. Rooke, Misses Emily and Ada, the white rookes, and Mrs. Fawcett, Mr. Peacocks, &c.

At sea. 'Danube.'

May 26, 1867.

Trade-wind blowing in our teeth. Weather cooler. No Divine Service. Men employed in shifting cargo, so as to trim the ship.

At sea. 'Danube.'

May 27, 1867.

Exchange addresses with Newcombe at his request. The Peruvian Major is very ill; something more than sea sickness. Play backgammon, as usual, with the Admiralty agent with alternate success.

At sea. 'Danube.'

May 28, 1867.

Good many Spaniards ill. Rough sea; head winds; stiff trades. Take a couple of pills without much effect. Knock off so many meat meals and confine self to fish and marmalade for breakfast; banana for luncheon; one dish meat at dinner. Play backgammon with Naval agent; dice against me. Draw a little, and write up diary a little. Read the 'Claverings' by Trollope. Port of cabin shut as water washes in on weather side. Number of berth 80 on starboard side, main-deck forward. Thermometer 84° F. in companion; still cooler on main-deck. Saloon hot and close, because shut up.

At sea. 'Danube.'

May 29, 1867.

Sea much calmer. Cargo ports open, scuttles, &c. Follow up the pills with a Seidlitz powder. Jolly cool on main-deck. The Peruvian Major is much worse; he now vomits blood, and before evening vomits coffee-grounds; a regular case of yellow Jack. He must have contracted the disease at Panama and brought it on board with him. There is little or no hope for him. The knowledge that yellow Jack is on board takes away the appetite of those who are fresh from England, and who have not had it.

At sea. 'Danube.' 'Atrato' off St. Peter Island.

May 30, 1867.

At 4 A.M. this morning the unfortunate Peruvian Major died of yellow fever. He was buried at 8 A.M., the Bishop and his Chaplain officiating, whilst in sight of Porto Rico. The death threw a gloom over the ship's company, which was, however, soon dissipated by the near view which we had of St. Thomas and the islands between there and St. Peter Island, where we arrived at 3.30 P.M., getting close alongside the starboard side of 'Atrato' steamer by 4 P.M. The 'Derwent,' commanded by Parkes, who was first of 'Tasmanian,' was on the other side of her. After dinner at 5 P.M., I went on board the 'Derwent' to see Parkes; and the 'Derwent' steamed away soon after for St. Thomas. The specie and cargo was first transferred, and then the passengers and luggage. I remained on board the 'Danube' till 11 P.M. and lights out; and then I went to look up my quarters with Morris in Nos. 141 and 142 berths forward in the saloon, badly ventilated and a peculiar smell, suggestive of every infectious disease.

St. Peter Island. 'Atrato' Steamer. At sea.

May 31, 1867.

At 6 A.M. we were off, steaming through the archipelago of small islands and rocks that are scattered in every direction; and by breakfast time were in blue water and out of sight of land. The scuttles of lower-deck are necessarily closed, and consequently we are nearly stifled below. The 'Atrato' is a fine vessel, but not so long as the 'Danube,' though of much greater beam. Her accommodation is very inferior, and comfort is not studied as on board the 'Danube.' At meal time we secure comfortable places, middle of table, starboard opposite Mr. Barton, and with Brown, Baker, Morris, Turnbull, and Tennent as neighbours. Play at ship's quoits before dinner. Delightful on deck. About 150 passengers. Great scramble at meals. Weather much cooler.

At sea. N. lat. 21° 24', W. long. 60° 33'. 'Atrato' Steamer.

June 1, 1867.

Called by bath-boy at 5.30 A.M. Get up and have a luxurious bath. Water much cooler. On deck till first bell for breakfast. Lieut.-Col. Langley, of the 16th, from Barbadoes, is on board with two dogs, three parrots, a turtle, wife and three children. The turtle is for the Duke of Cambridge. Luncheon is now at 8 bells and dinner at 4 P.M. Dancing in the forecastle among the sailors. Write up journal and ink in drawings in evening. Ex-President General Geffrard and Yankees, &c., playing at loo. The General seems to be frequently looed. Distance run 238 miles. Distance to the Lizard 3150 miles.

'Atrato' Steamer; at sea. N. lat. 24° 15', W. long. 57° 26'.

June 2, 1867.

Still calm sea. Divine service at 10.30, after mustering of the men on the quarter-deck. Capt. Rivett reads the service, and a parson on board preached. Read critique on Lord Lorne's book, 'Trip to the Tropics,' in the 'Times,' giving an account of ex-President Geffrard, who is a passenger on board here.

Champagne at dinner by my neighbours at dinner. The Duke of Cambridge's turtle dies. Examine net with curls on it, property of one of the Porto Rico Spaniards, which Posie brings for our examination. Turnbull walking about arm-in-arm with Miss Hill. Steel in his usual state. Distance run 252 miles; distance from Lizard 2898.

'Atrato' Steamer; at sea.   N. lat. 27° 18', W. long. 54° 18'.

June 3, 1867.

The yellow fever, I hear, has been so very bad at Port Royal that all the gunners had gone up to Newcastle. The battery lost its sergeant-major and several men. Charlie and Posie Tennent went out to Jamaica by the mail, early in February, under care of Miss Hill. They stay at Bournemouth. Distance run 256 miles; distance from Lizard 2643.

'Atrato' Steamer; at sea.   N. lat. 29° 56', W. long. 51°.

June 4, 1867.

Usual routine. Head wind. Water in bath beautifully cool at 5.30 A.M. Coffee at 6 A.M.; on deck till breakfast at 9 A.M. Play chess with Mr. Brown, and beat him in two games. Distance run 231 miles; distance from Lizard 2404 miles. Principal amusement of ex-President seems putting on new clothes every day. To see him with his spectacles down on his nose and his head tied up with a bandana, and a hat over all, fast asleep in an arm-chair, is a fine sight. He has avowed to twenty-two children.

'Atrato' Steamer; at sea.   N. lat. 32° 30', W. long. 47° 30'.

June 5, 1867.

Weather cooler; thermometer 70° Fahr. in companion. Distance run 247 miles; distance from Lizard 2151. Drawing all the morning. Draw the hawksbill turtle in fore saloon after luncheon with Posie. Charlie not well at dinner, and has to leave the table. After dinner he is better. Watch Spaniards playing at bull. After tea play "consequence" with Charlie, Posie, and Lily, and Miss Smith. Chess with Charlie, giving him a queen.

'Atrato' Steamer; at sea.   N. lat. 35° 20', W. long. 43° 30'.

June 6, 1867.

Wind abeam, going 11½ knots. Rather seedy. Lottery on ship's run, and Spaniards play cards on deck. Ashby wins the sweep. Distance run 269 miles; distance from Lizard Point 1888. Monte playing; little snob Perkins winning.

'Atrato' Steamer; at sea.   N. lat. 38° 19', W. long. 35° 43'.

June 7, 1867.

Calm sea. Water still cooler. Thermometer in hatch, 60°. Wind abeam, very light. Steaming well. Pass a large ship to the southward of us, steering same course as ourselves. Get the scuttle of cabin opened for first time. Parrots brought on deck for airing and sun. Pass a brigantine close to us, on same course. Play at hide-and-seek with children. Play at chess with old Brown, and beat him. Distance run 292 miles; distance from Lizard 1597.

'Atrato' Steamer; at sea. N. lat. 41°, W. long. 33° 44'.

June 8, 1867.

Fresh breeze from S. and by E. Steaming 12·6 knots. Stop engines for fifteen minutes to pack. More gambling in fore saloon. Distance run 282 miles; distance from Lizard 1315 miles. Posie wins the sweepstakes.

'Atrato' Steamer; at sea. N. lat. 43° 29', W. long. 27° 56'.

June 9, 1867.

At noon to-day we accomplished 304 miles, and are 1012 miles from the Lizard Point. Muster at 10.30 and Divine service. Mr. Turnbull in a bad temper with all of our party. Chat and walk with Charlie, and hear a great deal about himself, family, and cousin Posie. Pass large ship to leeward in morning.

'Atrato' Steamer; at sea.

June 10, 1867.

Fine calm sea, slight swell from N.E. Got up later than usual. Cold bath, and on deck till breakfast. Distance accomplished at noon 301 miles; Lizard Point distant 711 miles. The last of the bullocks slaughtered, and the house in which they had been kept removed from deck. Mr. Turnbull still in bad humour. Sleep and bask in sun all morning.

'Atrato' Steamer; at sea.

June 11, 1867.

Calm, warm morning; thermometer 70°. Dress in light clothing again. Distance accomplished only 282 miles. Distance to Lizard 429 miles, to Southampton 165; total 594 miles. Charlie's asthma very bad. Basking in the sun all day. Games with Posie and Aggy Chopin. In evening two games of chess with Mr. Brown.

'Atrato' Steamer; at sea.

June 12, 1867.

Breeze. Fine morning. Thermometer 56°. Pack of cards brought in morning 12s. 10d. Look out for Lizard. 165 miles to Southampton.

At sea. 'Atrato.' Southampton. Anglesey.

June 13, 1867.

England. 8.30 A.M. Needles? Southampton. Home again.

10, Terrace, Anglesey.

June 14, 1867.

Report myself to Officer commanding 12th Brigade Royal Artillery, Fort Brockhurst.

FINIS.

APPENDIX.

THE first opportunity of bringing the Nicaragua Railway scheme before the English public was at the Meeting of the British Association at Dundee, which commenced on the 4th September, 1867.

Dundee.

September 5, 1867.

Fine morning. Bathe in the public baths at the Docks. After breakfast attend the Sectional meeting; Sir S. Baker, &c. As Captain Wilson has failed to make his appearance, I am selected to commence the proceedings with my paper and Maury's.

·

BRITISH ASSOCIATION, DUNDEE.

THURSDAY, SEPTEMBER 5, 1867.

The work of the Sections commenced to-day with various lucid addresses from the Presidents. Of these Sir Samuel Baker's was the greatest attraction, and drew a very large audience. An instructive account of an exploration in Nicaragua, by Lieutenant Oliver, was also given in the Geographical Section. Sir Samuel took a gloomy view of Livingstone's fate, but praised Sir Roderick Murchison and the Government for their action.

· SECTION E.—GEOGRAPHY AND ETHNOLOGY.

IN THE ALBERT INSTITUTE.

President.—Sir Samuel Baker, F.R.G.S.

Vice-Presidents.—Sir James E. Alexander, K.C.L.S., Admiral Sir Edw. Belcher, John Crawfurd, F.R.S., Col. Sir Henry James, R.E., F.R.S., Sir John Lubbock, Bart., F.R.S., Sir Roderick Murchison, Bart., F.R.S., Admiral E. Ommanney, C.B., Gen. Sir A. S. Waugh, F.R.S.

Secretaries.—H. W. Bates, Assist.-Sec. R.G.S., Cyril C. Graham, F.R.G.S., Clements R. Markham, F.R.G.S., S. J. Mackie, F.G.S., R. Sturrock.

Committee.—Prof. D. T. Ansted, F.R.S., John Arrowsmith, F.R.G.S., Sir David Baxter, Bart., W. E. Baxter, M.P., H. G. Bohn, F.R.G.S., Sir John Bowring, LL.D., Bishop of Brechin, W. Brand, George Busk, F.R.S., C. Holt Bracebridge, F.R.G.S., Dr. P. O'Callaghan, D.C.L., LL.D., Dr. Cuthbert Collingwood, M.D., F.L.S., Robert Dunn, F.R.C.S., V.P.E.S., Dr. Davie, Sir Walter Elliot, F.L.S., General Sir Vincent Eyre, K.C.S.I., C.B., James Ferguson, F.R.S., Rev. Dr. Ginsburg, H. Gourlay, Dr. James Hunt, Pres. A.S.L., M. N. de Khanikof, Prof. Alfred Newton, M.A., F.L.S., Sir J. Ogilvy, Bart., M.P., Lieut. S. P. Oliver, R.A., Sir Arthur Phayre, Col. R. L. Playfair, F.R.G.S., John Ramsay, J. Sydney Smith, F.R.G.S., Rev. H. B. Tristram, F.L.S., James White, James Yeaman.

DIRECT COMMUNICATION FROM THE ATLANTIC TO THE PACIFIC.

Lieut. S. P. Oliver, of the Royal Artillery, F.R.G.S., at the request of the Chairman, read a paper giving a description of two routes through Nicaragua. Various routes, he said, have been proposed by eminent engineers and geographers across the great American isthmus, at intervals during the last twenty years, all more or less practicable, from the Tehuantepec route on the north to the Darien Canal and Humboldt's Atrato River Route on the south. Of all these, the only actual line in operation is between Panama and Aspinwall, at present so successfully worked by an energetic American company since 1855. Of the others, the only routes that can at all compete with the Panama Railroad are those through Nicaragua. One of these has been, and is partially, worked, though unsuccessfully, by the Transit Route *viâ* the river San Juan and the Lake. The other, soon likely to be carried out, is that proposed by Captain Pim, R.N., for a railway. The first of the two last-mentioned routes has been more than once advocated as suitable for water communication (indeed, even for a ship canal) from the Atlantic to the Pacific, in 1850. The last, which has more recently attracted attention, has been prevented only by want of sufficient capital to carry out the terms of the local Government concession. Both these routes, he said, necessarily follow the configuration of the valley through the elsewhere uninterrupted chain of impracticable Cordilleras, and it was therefore necessary that he should briefly allude to the physical geography of the country immediately surrounding the Nicaraguan lakes. Lieutenant Oliver then gave a description of the Nicaraguan country. To give an idea of the difficulties of the navigation of the San Juan, against which the Transit Company have to contend, he gave a description of his journey up that river. Leaving behind them the harbour of San Juan del Norte, or Greytown, with its dangerous bar frequented with sharks, Lieut. Oliver and his party steamed up the still waters of the San Juan. The steamer in which they were, only drawing about eighteen inches of water, at first went along well, but soon scraping over shallows, poling off the banks, and shoving off from snags, &c., showed them what they had to expect. The next morning they found themselves hard and fast on a bank, about fourteen miles from Greytown. After much time lost in vainly endeavouring to get off, they had to take to flat-bottomed boats and canoes, and pull and sail, under a burning sun, to the divergence of the San Juan with the main stream, or Colorado mouth of the river, about nineteen miles from Greytown, where they found another steamer waiting for them, and had to remain till the evening of the 18th of February, bringing up the cargo of the other steamer piecemeal. Here they observed the remains of a futile attempt made a few years ago to dam up the Colorado branch, in order to divert the stream down the San Juan branch—a stupendous undertaking. The low banks and marshes of the delta are such that the closing of the Colorado would cause the flooding of the surrounding country. The Lieutenant thought that it was more than probable that eventually a more direct and easy route may yet be found up the valley of the San Juan, across the mountains to the tablelands of Costa Rica and San José. He hoped this would soon be effected, especially as he believed Captain Pim proposed personally to explore this unknown river. From San Carlos, the regular transit route, as at present carried out, is a paddle steamer to Virgin Bay, sixty miles, then across the narrow neck of land, twelve miles, to San Juan del Sur, making the total length of this route, from ocean to ocean, 165 miles. Lieutenant Oliver then gave a detailed description of his

journey through the country. On the 28th of March he and his friends started off to follow the party under Mr. Collinson, which was cutting its way through the woods to the Rama River. They had been cutting a whole month, so that they had made considerable progress. Their party consisted of Lieutenant Oliver himself and five Spanish Americans, with Eusebio, a native of San Miguel, as guide. The cutting, called by the Spaniards El Picquet, commenced at the very shore of the lake at San Miguelito. The pathway being bored out at intervals as required for the levelling and survey, did not make the tract a difficult one to follow; but for the first seven miles, over savannah and jicaral, they found it a better course to follow the regular cattle-route to the outermost rancho. They therefore skirted the foot of some hills to the north, through occasional thickets of bamboo, and halted first outside the denser forests at the last station, where water was procurable in a grove of stately corso palm. The mosquitos drove them nearly mad in the night; and at early daylight they were glad to be off, entering the cutting into the vast and hitherto impenetrable forests of the Mosquito frontier. The path travelled through this part of the cutting was in many places very difficult for the oxen with corones to pass, and frequent halts took place in order to shift the corones and rest the beasts. On the 7th May they came in sight of Captain Pim and his party, who had come in search of them. He accompanied them to their last camp, and at once dispatched a pitpan full of provisions up to the party still left behind. They proceeded in canoe on the 8th down to the Rama station, where the bulk of the stores were deposited, and, leaving all rapids, found themselves in the navigable waters of the Rama River, reaching the village of Rama Indiana by night. Here Collinson returned to finish his survey; and Lieutenant Oliver's presence being no longer required, he accompanied Captain Pim down the Rama River to the Atlantic, proceeding on the 9th to Greytown by canoe. Of the engineering details of this line, he said it was not his province to speak. Mr. Collinson's report would soon appear in full, when he would do away with many erroneous ideas that prevail about the course passed over. However, too much credit, he affirmed, could not be given to Collinson and Mr. Deering for the perseverance, energy, and courage with which they prosecuted their survey in the face of more than ordinary difficulties.

Mr. CRAWFURD said that Lieutenant Oliver had, no doubt, had excellent opportunities of forming an opinion upon the comparison between the red men of America and the black men of Africa, as he had seen them in Madagascar. He would like to know which of these races Lieutenant Oliver preferred.

Lieutenant OLIVER. I think that is a very difficult question indeed.

Mr. CRAWFURD. That is just the reason why I put it. (Laughter.)

Lieutenant OLIVER was sorry he had given that subject very little of his attention; but he might say that the men who were with him, and who were their best men when cutting through the forests, were men from Africa, whose ancestors had been imported as slaves several hundreds of years ago to some island in the West Indies. They made themselves troublesome there, and were placed by some Government (whether English or Spanish he did not know) on the coast of Mosquito. Ever since that they had followed the occupation of mahogany-cutters, and there were no better men in the world. The Indians there were a useless set; they had, perhaps, never been developed. They followed hunting, shooting, and fishing, and all they cared for was to provide for their physical wants. During the dry season they laid up provisions for use during the wet season, and that seemed to be the utmost of their

desires. The black men with whom he had been acquainted in Madagascar were also widely different from the negroes he met with in Africa. The people with whom he had most to do in Madagascar were of the dominant race, and were of a superior class.

Mr. CRAWFURD. You saw a great many monkeys and a great many savages. Did you encounter anything like the missing link between man and the monkeys? (Laughter.)

Lieutenant OLIVER. No, certainly not. (Renewed laughter.)

Mr. CRAWFURD. I see you have been eating lizards and iguanas. What like is iguana flesh?

Lieutenant OLIVER. Iguana flesh is like what I would imagine the flesh of a young child would be. (Laughter.)

Mr. CRAWFURD. Did you like it?

Lieutenant OLIVER. Well, we were generally pretty hard up when we ate it. (Laughter.)

Mr. CRAWFURD. You would not have eaten a young child, I suppose, in the same circumstances?

Lieutenant OLIVER (laughing). Well, I don't know (Laughter.)

Admiral OMMANNEY asked Lieutenant Oliver's opinion as to the harbours for the accommodation of vessels that might be formed at the ends of the proposed line.

Lieutenant OLIVER said the engineering question was almost taken out of his hands, and he believed that other papers would be read on that subject during the present meeting; but he knew that two harbours were proposed by the engineers—one at Monkey Point, on the east coast, which would be well sheltered from the only dangerous winds that prevailed in that place, and the other at Realejo, on the west, at which there was a splendid bay, capable of sheltering a large fleet.

The CHAIRMAN remarked that the question put by Admiral Ommanney was one of very great importance, as, without suitable harbours, such a line could be of little service. The want of such harbours had been felt in the cases both of the Isthmus of Suez and of the Isthmus of Panama, and he was therefore delighted to hear that in the present instance this difficulty was likely to be overcome. He had no doubt, if this work was undertaken by Captain Bedford Pim, it would prove one of the greatest engineering works that had ever been executed. He moved a hearty vote of thanks to Lieutenant Oliver for the able and interesting paper he had read. (Applause.)

The second opportunity occurred at an early meeting of the Royal Geographical Society. Sir Roderick Murchison, the venerable President, in his opening address at the commencement of the session, alluded to the exploration as follows:—

"Among the papers which have been received at our office, and will be read to you at the earlier meetings of the session, I may observe that some of the most important, in a geographical point of view, relate to different portions of the isthmus of Central America, and to surveys which have had for their object the discovery of lines of traverse, whether for railways or ship canals, between the Atlantic and Pacific Oceans. One of these papers is by Mr. Collinson, a young engineer employed in the exploration of a line of route across the wildest parts of Nicaragua, in which he was engaged under the direction of Captain Bedford Pim, R.N., and which may be expected to throw much light on the physical geography of that region. On this subject, but more particularly relating to the winds and currents of the sea-coasts of Nicaragua, an interesting paper was read by Captain Maury

before the Geographical Section of the British Association at Dundee ; and I may venture to hope that this distinguished hydrographer will communicate to us a memoir on the same subject in the course of the Session.

"Another memoir, by M. de Puydt, on that portion of the Isthmus of Darien which lies about 60 miles to the southward of the tract reported upon, some sixteen years ago, by Mr. Gisborne, will doubtless excite much interest, particularly as the author shows that the dividing ridge betweenthe Atlantic and Pacific Oceans there attains a maximum of only 120 feet above the sea-level."

THE ROYAL GEOGRAPHICAL SOCIETY.

Session 1867–68.

Second Meeting, 25th November, 1867.

THE NICARAGUA TRANSIT ROUTE.

At a crowded and distinguished meeting of the Royal Geographical Society, on Monday evening, Sir Roderick Impey Murchison, Bart. (President), in the chair—present, Earl Granville, Viscount Milton, M.P., Viscount Strangford, Sir Geo. Pollock, Gen. Lefroy, Right Hon. Sir J. Pakington, Admiral Collinson, the Hydrographer of the Admiralty, Capt. S. Osborn, Mr. Crawfurd, the Astronomer Royal, Capt. A. Young, besides a great number of leading gentlemen and others—a most interesting and valuable account of recent explorations in Nicaragua, carried out with a view to open up an interoceanic transit through that country, was given by Mr. John Collinson, C.E., F.R.S., who had just returned from the triumphant execution of the work, having completed the only spirit-level survey ever made across Central America, with the exception of that of the Panama Railway.

The President, in introducing Mr. Collinson, called attention to the fact that very many efforts had been made to penetrate across the primeval forest which characterizes the various narrowings of the great isthmus of Central America ; but from the paper which would be read that evening they would see that this effort differed materially from all others, inasmuch as it was eminently successful, and he could speak of it as unexampled for hardships overcome and for the success it had attained. Mr. Collinson, on rising, was received with applause. He then read a highly instructive and exhaustive account of his expedition, and was listened to with marked attention throughout. The following is an abstract:—

The paper, entitled 'Explorations in Central America,' contains a part of the history of a grand enterprise, inaugurated in the year 1860 by Captain Bedford Pim, with the view to establish a healthy, economical, and safe transit across the isthmus of the New World. One route already exists in working order (the Panama Railway), but, from its inefficiency to meet the requirements of the rapidly-increasing isthmian traffic, from the insecurity of its terminal ports, from the deadly climate of the country it traverses, and from the exorbitant charges of its managers, the want of a competing line has been long felt as a growing necessity. Many routes have been proposed, both for canals and railways, but all projects for the former have been found too costly to offer a chance of fair remuneration to investors. As regards the latter, many have been proposed, and are even now proposed; but, from certain physical features of the isthmus, the route projected by Capt. Pim across Nicaragua has stood the test of practical examination in a more satisfactory manner than any of the others. On the Caribbean Sea its proposed terminal port is a bay opening to the south, situated under the lee of Monkey Point

and two small islands. It is about four miles across, with an average depth of $3\frac{1}{2}$ fathoms. On the Pacific the option of two ports exists—Realejo, too well and favourably known to require comment on, and a snug though small harbour, San Juan del Sur. In the intervening tract of country lie the two great lakes of Nicaragua and Managua, which have covered up and obliterated all except the highest peaks on the central line of the grand range of the Cordilleras, leaving two subsidiary ranges of low altitude on either side, one dividing the water-shed of the Caribbean Sea and the lakes, the other that of the lakes and the Pacific. The tract of country lying between the latter, much of it cultivated and thickly settled, has been repeatedly examined and surveyed for canal and railway purposes, and reported favourably upon for the latter; but the other tract, lying between Lake Nicaragua and the Caribbean Sea, uninhabited and covered by dense primeval forests and jungle, had never been explored, even partially, until 1863. In that year he went out with Capt. Pim and surveyed about 30 miles from Monkey Point inland; another party at the same time attempted the remaining section to the lake, but after bravely struggling for some months had to succumb without attaining their object. In 1865 another attempt was made on this *terra incognita* by a party commanded by an American backwoodsman, who had distinguished himself in the defeat of Walker, but he likewise failed. In January of this year, at the instance of certain American capitalists (among others Mr. Webb, the builder of the Dunderberg) interested in Capt. Pim's project, he was induced to undertake the survey of this section, so as to complete the proof, if possible, of the practicability of the entire route; and on February 25 he commenced operations from the lake end, with two Englishmen and an average of a dozen natives as assistants. His previous experience had enabled him to draw deductions as to the topography of the country, which he found invaluable as guides by which to select the best route. On the one side an important river, the Rama, though with many turnings, seemed to run a pretty nearly east course, and emptied itself into the ocean about 11 miles south of Monkey Point. Almost on the same parallel, another river, the Tule, emptied itself into the lake, and evidently drew its life from the dividing ridge, where the true summit level must exist. He therefore worked as closely as he could up the valley of one river and down that of the other; and though, in this preliminary exploration, he was only able to go blindly ahead, without much choice of track, he succeeded in crossing the summit level at so low an altitude as 619 feet above, and at a distance of $31\frac{3}{4}$ miles from the lake. The gradients laid down from point to point are very good, the worst being for a short distance 1 in 80; and he is confident that these can be preserved without heavy earthworks. The rock, wherever apparent, is always volcanic, basalt, porphyry, and tufa; and this rock, except on the tops of the hills, is covered with a yellowish earth, sometimes friable, and sometimes taking the consistency of clay, and in the deeper valleys forming a soft conglomerate, with large masses of flint embedded. This yellow subsoil, formed by the degradation of the rock, is covered in its turn by a rich loam formed of roots and decayed vegetable matter, and, well watered by tropical showers, is astonishingly fertile. On June 2 he succeeded in effecting a junction with his old work at a distance of $62\frac{1}{2}$ miles from the lake, and thus completing the survey, establishing durable bench marks, and carrying levels from lake to ocean. The results have proved that the country admits of an economical line being constructed; and a further careful examination, with more time and means at disposal, will doubtless reveal opportunities of effecting great improvements on the present one as laid out. The conclusion of the paper, which occupied forty minutes in reading, was much applauded.

The PRESIDENT said, as Englishmen, they must all be proud of Mr. Collinson, a civil engineer who had shown so much skill and perseverance in surmounting the difficulties of this original survey of a wild country, and had laid before them geographical data of considerable importance. He would first call upon Captain Bedford Pim, who was the original projector of this traverse of the Isthmus, and who had previously distinguished himself by his researches in the Arctic regions.

Captain BEDFORD PIM said the able paper of Mr. Collinson left him hardly scope for saying a word upon the subject. There was one point it might be desirable to mention, which was, that Mr. Collinson's feat was absolutely the first spirit-level survey across Central America, with the exception of that undertaken for the Panama Railway. He had great pleasure in bearing testimony to the ability of Mr. Collinson. Few people were aware of the amount of hardship and difficulty met with in cutting through the dense forests of Nicaragua. Mr. Collinson surmounted every obstacle with a degree of bravery and perseverance which deserved high praise; and had it not been for his great exertions he (Capt. Pim) should have had to return to England for the third time disappointed in opening up this hitherto unknown tract of country. Lieutenant Oliver of the Royal Artillery, already well and favourably known to this Society, was also entitled to much credit for the able manner in which he assisted Mr. Collinson in the traverse from the lake to the shores of the Atlantic.

Commodore MAURY (U.S.N.), after acknowledging the great services which Captain Pim had rendered to the commerce of the world by projecting and carrying out the Nicaragua route, observed that he had rendered no less a service to geographical science. He and his able assistants had made us acquainted with the geography of these regions, and given us an amount of information which we never possessed before. He (Captain Maury) was of opinion that the Nicaragua route would be preferable to the Panama one for crossing to the Pacific. All that country was liable to what are called periodical rains. A belt of cloud might be considered as extending in these latitudes from the coast of Africa across the Atlantic to the shores of America. This cloud-belt moved from north to south with the sun in declination. It went as far south as lat. 3°. When it came north it passed over Panama and Mexico, and was the source of the periodical rains in those regions. But the effect was the annual occurrence of a long period of calm in the Pacific near Panama, which rendered that part difficult of access by sailing vessels, an objection which did not apply to the ports of Nicaragua, where these calms are unknown. When he was in Mexico two years ago he had the honour of calling the attention of the Emperor Maximilian to the subject of investigating the phenomena of this cloud-belt, with its accompanying rainy season. His Majesty, with that enlightenment which was his characteristic, authorized him to procure instruments from London, with a view to the establishment of not less than 62 meteorological observatories in Mexico, which were placed under the direction of the Geographical Society of that country. He was surprised to find this Mexican Society in so flourishing a condition. For many years, notwithstanding the revolutions in that country, it had been pursuing its quiet work, publishing its journals from time to time, and holding regularly its meetings. He could not tell what had become of the instruments; but he thought it was worthy the attention of the Council of the Royal Geographical Society of London whether they would not open a correspondence with the Mexican Society, with the view of obtaining from them the observations which these instruments were sent to procure.

Admiral Sir EDWARD BELCHER said, perhaps as surveyor of the whole of the

Pacific coast of Central America, a word from him might not be unimportant. He questioned if any of the persons who had spoken had any personal knowledge of that coast, or of the climate, the winds, or the facility of travelling along the coast. When he was there he never had any difficulty in getting in and out of the Bay of Panama. He was glad to hear that a route had been surveyed across Nicaragua; but he thought the proposed line started from an awkward part of the coast on the Atlantic or eastern side, where there was great difficulty in effecting a landing. It would not be easy to find anchorage for ships; neither was there any harbour on the opposite or Pacific side; and the frequent gales of wind on that coast termed Papagayos would dismast any ship that attempted to approach it from seaward under canvas. A little to the southward there was a splendid harbour, perfectly free from gales. If the party had run their line further to the south-west, through Costa Rica, they would have found a fine country. On the other hand, in the Bay of Honduras, a line had been examined by Mr. Squiers, many years ago, and found to be practicable; while the Gulf of Fonseca to the southward, where that line terminates, would contain the whole navy of England. On these accounts he would have preferred a more northerly line through Honduras—a country infinitely richer in every way than Nicaragua, with a better climate, and perfectly free from those insect pests which were found further south. With respect to the communication between Colon and Panama, he never heard till this evening that there was any difficulty in landing at Colon; and on the Panama side, from 1837 to 1840, he was in the habit of sending the 'Starling' tender, under Captain Kellett, backwards and forwards with despatches, with such certainty that he knew almost to a day when he would arrive. All the accounts about the difficulties of the Bay of Panama he could not comprehend, for he never experienced bad weather or a gale of wind there in his life.

Commander Peacock said he had surveyed the coast of Nicaragua as far back as 1831, and had the honour of discovering that the coast-line had been laid down 58 miles of longitude in error on all the maps and charts previous to that time, which was afterwards verified by Capt. Owens, R.N., in H.M. surveying-ship 'Blossom' in 1832, as the discovery was considered so important that the Commander-in-Chief ordered this ship to proceed to the Mosquito coast on purpose to ascertain the truth of this extraordinary error, which had remained for upwards of *three centuries* in all the maps and charts of the world. This coast was discovered by the immortal Columbus in the month of September, 1502, when on his fourth voyage. Mr. Peacock had also had the honour of surveying the Isthmus of Panama from ocean to ocean, and of commanding the first steam-ship that ever visited Panama, in February 1842. He also had the honour of calling attention, in 1831, to the route across Lake Nicaragua by steamers of light draft and by railway to St. Juan del Sur; and his letter on the subject would be found in the archives of the Admiralty, with this comment—"Should the *west* coast of Nicaragua be laid down correctly, the eastern coast being so much in error, the distance across to the Pacific would, by this singular discovery, be 60 miles shorter than hitherto supposed by geographers." Mr. Shepherd told him that he had taken a schooner drawing 6 feet of water up the Colorado branch of the river to Lake Nicaragua; and also that the ground between the lake and St. Juan del Sur was very easy for carrying a railway across. He (Mr. Peacock) had also explored the river St. Juan to its junction with the Colorado branch, and could endorse all that Mr. Collinson had stated in the able and interesting paper they had had the pleasure of listening to, in respect of climate and the numbers of jaguars, alligators, &c. met with in the jungle and on the banks of the rivers on that coast. In the letter he had had the honour of addressing to

Admiral Colpoys in November 1831, he named an excellent suggestion of Mr. Shepherd's, viz., that if the Colorado branch of the St. Juan were to be dammed across, at its confluence with the latter, falling into the harbour of St. Juan, he believed it would scour a deep water-channel from thence into the harbour, and enable vessels of some draught to ascend at once to the lake. With respect to the remark made by Mr. Collinson as to large vessels having been said to have ascended the St. Juan in the early voyages of the Spaniards, it is not improbable that the Colorado branch may be comparatively of *recent* origin, which would account for the shallow condition of the St. Juan itself at this time, for the hydrographical changes that have taken place ever since 1831, by the growing out of Point Arenas upwards of 1½ mile in length in less than 30 years, is one of the most remarkable changes, by natural causes, known; for what was a good harbour from 1831 to 1857, with anchorage for a fleet of large ships, having deep water on both sides of this natural dyke, became converted into a lagoon in 1859, by the spit joining the mainland, soon after which the harbour was shut up[*]. Capt. Freeman of the sloop 'Countess of Belmore,' employed in the shell-turtle fishery on that coast, told Capt. Peacock that rich mines of gold and silver existed a few days' journey inland from Blewfields to the northward of St. Juan, which doubtless were those known as the Chontales mines.

Dr. Seemann would speak as to the feeders of the projected railway; he had twice explored the greater part of Nicaragua under the direction of Capt. Pim. His route lay from Leon north-eastwards. After leaving Leon, and for four or five days' journey, the climate gradually became delightfully fine. He went up as far as the boundary of Honduras, and found there extensive mining operations going on, the ore being chiefly of silver. He then went southward to Chontales, the new gold region, which had been brought into notice by Capt. Pim. The climate of the Pacific side of Nicaragua is comparatively dry, and the rainy season short. After passing to the east of the lake the rainy season becomes prolonged several months, the rains continuing till February, while in other parts they cease in November. The vegetation on the Pacific side is similar to that near Panama; but at Chontales it is much more luxuriant, and the timber there is finer than it is on the Pacific side. The whole of the Chontales forest is a virgin forest. At his suggestion a meeting had lately been held in Chontales to ascertain the possibility of cutting a route from Chontales to the Blewfields settlement. He had found that several people had made their way to the coast; and he was glad to say that a route was now being cut under the direction of Colonel Maury, and by order of the Javali Company.

Mr. J. H. Murchison observed that Admiral Belcher, while speaking of the Honduras route, had forgotten that no proper survey had been made across Honduras; whilst at Nicaragua a most elaborate and able survey had been carried out. More than that, a transit route had already been in operation across Nicaragua to St. Juan del Sur. Another circumstance in favour of the route proposed by Mr. Collinson was that the United States Government, about two years ago, had sent a staff of engineers to survey the Atlantic coast of Central America, under the charge of Captain West, who, after pronouncing the harbour of Greytown impracticable, and making a special survey of the harbour at Monkey Point, had stated that this was the harbour on the Atlantic which could be made the most practicable for commercial

---

[*] See Plan of Port St. Juan surveyed by Mr. Peacock in 1831, with the gradual growth of the spit from year to year up to December 1858, in the Map Collection of the Royal Geographical Society.

purposes. Again, the climate was finer than at the Isthmus of Panama, and the distance from New York and Liverpool to San Francisco, by the Nicaragua route, was considerably shorter than by the Panama or the Honduras route.

The BISHOP OF HONOLULU said he had made several transits over the Isthmus of Panama, and could not concur in the ground taken by the advocates of the Nicaragua route, viz., that the one over Panama was unhealthy. In 1862 he stayed *most part of a week* there with his wife and children, and two clergymen with their families, and they found the place healthy, and suffered no inconvenience. The intelligent consul there, Mr. Henderson, had often said, as a *tropical* climate, that of Panama city *was one of the very best*, and that he enjoyed there very good health. At Aspinwall or Colon, on the Atlantic side, the manager of the railway, who had had an experience of above ten years' residence there, with his family, said, "if a person took the proper precautions usual in the tropics, and was careful about stimulants, for example, he might live as long there as anywhere else." The chaplain had told him (the Bishop) the same. He mentioned these facts in vindication of the Panama railway route, from whose managers he (the Bishop) had ever received much personal kindness and attention.

Admiral OMMANNEY said he was stationed off the coast of Central America in command of H.M.S. 'Brunswick,' 80 guns, for five months, most of that time lying off Colon, and could confirm all that the Bishop had just said as to the salubrity of Colon and the advantages of the Panama railway. The climate of that locality when the railway was first commenced was in bad repute; since then it had improved, owing to the clearance of timber and vegetation along a belt of country on each side of the line through the dense virgin frost which covers the Isthmus: thus the prevailing wind which blows from the N.E. direct from the sea over Colon renders *that place healthy*. His ship's company, consisting of upwards of 800 persons, enjoyed good health; he had the satisfaction to leave the station without the loss of a man by death from the climate. The present survey of Nicaragua, with regard to opening out an access into that country, was a good work accomplished, and reflected very great credit on those who had conquered the difficulties and privations: any work tending to develop the natural sources of wealth in Central America was a benefit to mankind. The proposed line as a means of interoceanic communication between the Atlantic and Pacific would be of little value unless there were good ports at each terminus capable of receiving the largest passenger ships: on this point he was sceptical. He had visited the Mosquito coast, and feared that no harbour existed at Monkey Point suitable for the object. He considered it a dangerous coast and subject to boisterous weather; he was once caught off Monkey Point on a lee-shore with a heavy gale, in a line-of-battle-ship; had difficulty to work off under storm-sails, aided by steam-power, against the heavy sea rolling along the coast. The advantage of the short transit by the existing Panama line, which has good towns at each terminus, would command the preference for passengers to the more lengthened route by the proposed scheme.

Mr. COLLINSON, in reply, adverted only to one point—the harbour at Monkey Point. He had had considerable experience of that harbour as to shelter. In 1863, in one of the most violent northers on that coast, he was for three days in that harbour, in one of the Royal Mail steamers, and was completely sheltered. On the contrary, at Colon, during one of these northers, the Royal Mail steamer 'Avon' was blown right on shore against the landing stage, which was entirely destroyed. She could not get out with full steam on.

The meeting then adjourned.

WOOLWA VOCABULARY.

Woolwa	English	Woolwa	English
Libra.	Woolwa people.	Ahmakouting.	Sleeping.
Wahi.	Brother.	Meouhka ahma-	To sleep.
Al.	Man.	kouting.	
Yel.	Woman.	Toonik.	Head.
Sirou backar.	Girl.	Tas.	Cloth to wear round
Al backar.	Boy.		the loins.
Backar.	Young.	Kalki.	Foot.
Yalki.	Wife.	Kinki.	Hand.
Alkimuk.	Husband.	Wakki.	Plantains.
Pamki.	Tapir.	Inkkini.	Bananas.
Nowarpowka.	Red tiger.	Um.	Corn.
Powka.	Red.	Sussunka.	Beads.
Nowar.	Tiger.	Simming.	Fish-hooks.
Nowar bulka.	Spotted tiger.	Sooksuwookka.	Cord.
Nowar burruska.	Black tiger.	Asnar.	Cloth.
Bulka.	Spotted.	Soobba.	Pot.
Burruska.	Black.	Watikah.	Banana bird.
Pichea.	White.	Veeah.	Hare.
Sunna.	Deer.	Kee.	Rock.
Sowie.	Wari.	Sou.	Ground.
Cassi.	To eat.	Souassung.	World.
Caskouting.	Eating.	Nowal.	Devil.
Deekoting.	Drinking.	Waikou.	A god.
Soopokouting.	Sucking.	Mah.	Sun.
Deeko.	To drink.	Walkoo.	Moon.
Yappoo.	Alligator.	Mahbruska.	Sky.
Kahama.	Iguana.	Waslouti.	Rain.
Was.	Water.	Ewi.	To die.
I warra.	Come here.	Yowahkooting.	To walk.
Baina warra.	Come here quick.	Yoolbutiang.	To talk.
Yowanakou.	Let us go.	Mahdi.	To-day.
Koorring.	Canoe.	Yun.	To-morrow.
Wahinah.	Paddle.	Dummi.	Yesterday.
Koobil.	Knife.	Koo.	Fire.
Sroban.	Bow and arrows.	Koolaka.	Firewood.
Keeddak.	Axe.	Pun.	Wood.
Oorrus.	Monkey.	Quassika.	Hammock.
Wummi.	Curassow.	Keettung.	Waterfall.
Wunkuruman.	Guan.	Tookwunnah.	Big.
Woomalo.	Partridge.	Was.	River.
Moolakoos.	Peccary.	Tooki.	Mouth.
Yamka.	Good.	Meekduka.	Eyes.
Dootka.	Bad.	Anaki.	Teeth.
Awai.	Yes.	Tapahki.	Ears.
Aissou.	None.	Bas.	Hair.
Eessou.	No.	Ki.	Mine.
Yungdecki.	Yours.	Waya hal.	Mosquito man.
Washbiloo.	Mishla.	Waya yel.	„ woman.
Mohiwah deakena.	His.	Souhtuk.	Calabash.
Amiseeka.	Sister.	Mahbootoring	Fighting.
Passinka.	Father.	Koomah.	Salt.
Mamaka.	Mother.	Koomhoo.	Rabbit.
Kahaloo.	Shirt.	Backar kee.	Children.
Kahasong.	Trowsers.	Oo.	House.
Coocoo.	Cocoa-nut.	Assun.	Hill.
Almuk.	Male.		
Tooroo.	Cattle.	Aslar.	One.
Panka.	Horse.	Bou.	Two.
Boorroo.	Donkey.	Bas.	Three.
Mulah.	Mule.	Aroonea.	Four.
Malaka.	Indian rabbit.	Seenca.	Five.
Kookuuik.	Armadillo.	Deeeea.	Six.
Hoombooka.	Bird.	Veeea.	Seven.
Ooli.	Turtle.	Bachea.	Eight.
Taspool.	India-rubber.	Tingnicaslar.	Nine.
Deehlatookuting.	Cooking.	Tingniskoobou.	Ten.
Pun.	Tree.		

MOSQUITO VOCABULARY.

Narra bal.	Come here.	Pies.	Eat.
Eine.	Make haste.	Ploom.	Victuals.
Kaiser.	Let us go.	Dies.	Drink.
Douce.	Stick.	Lia.	Water.
Yerri.	Long.	Lia Kowta.	Cold Water.
Clucki.	Cut.	Wano.	Come along.
Brebal.	Bring it here.	Apia.	No.
Yany.	Mine.	Aou.	Yes.
Man.	Your.	Yabra.	North.
Eisiken.	Father.	Blanco.	South.
Yapti.	Mother.	N'emopera.	Go this side.
Mooine.	Eldest brother.	Passer.	Wind.
Deevra.	Youngest brother.	Keero.	Knife.
Lakreka.	Sister.	Rakboos.	Gun.
Tahte.	Uncle.		
Yapti deevra.	Aunt.	Kumi.	One.
Damer.	Grandfather.	Wal.	Two.
Koohah.	Grandmother.	Yumpa.	Three.
Pearker.	Widow.	Waiwalun.	Four.
Mair.	Wife.	Matasip.	Five.
Mair waikna.	Husband.	Mata Walkaby.	Six.
Mairen.	Woman.	Mata Walkabykumi.	Seven.
Waikna.	Man.	Matawal wal.	Eight.
Lilla.	Mistress.	Matawal yumpa.	Nine.
Almuks.	Old man.	Matawal sip.	Ten.
Hupla.	People.	Youan eiske.	Twenty.
Mehi.	Friends.	Youan eiske wal.	Forty.

POSTSCRIPT.

THE PANAMA CANAL SCHEME.

[From the '*Globe*,' Monday, August 25, 1879.]

"As the result of inquiries at the State Department, and an interview with the President on the 7th inst. (writes a Washington correspondent of the 'New York Times'), it can be authoritatively stated that no action has been taken and no correspondence held by this Government either with regard to the Lesseps canal scheme in its relation to our foreign policy or with regard to the further exploration of the isthmus by another Government expedition, with a view to the organization of an American Canal Company. As far as the De Lesseps scheme is concerned, both the President and the Secretary of State are firmly convinced that no exigency is likely to arise which can cause disquietude or make it necessary for the Government to take steps for the protection of American interests. They believe that M. de Lesseps and the Paris Congress have selected an impracticable route, and that the Lesseps scheme will eventually fail through lack of financial support and for want of American cooperation. The report that another Government expedition to the isthmus is contemplated seems to be founded on a misapprehension. No such proposal has been made, and no such expedition thought of. Admiral Ammen, however, is very anxious that a Commission of American engineers should be appointed to make a careful examination and report upon the

whole subject of an interoceanic canal, with a view to further action should it then seem advisable. Many expeditions have explored the isthmus, and an immense mass of information relating thereto has been accumulated; and this information has never, in Admiral Ammen's opinion, been thoroughly and impartially examined and collated by a body of competent engineers. Such a body, he proposes, should now be organized by the Government, and if this Commission shall decide that the information already extant is insufficient, and report in favour of further exploration of any particular route, an expedition may be sent out for that purpose. As yet no action has been taken by the Government upon Admiral Ammen's proposal; but there is little doubt that it will be favourably considered, and that the Commission of United States engineers will be appointed.

"Secretary Thompson has received a letter from Admiral Ammen with regard to the proposed visit of Civil Engineer Ménocal to Nicaragua. The Admiral says:—'Should the Department grant the request of the Nicaraguan Government to permit Civil Engineer A. G. Ménocal, United States Navy, to go to that country for the purpose of improving the navigation of the San Juan river, in the vicinity of the Costillo Rapids, I would suggest that he be informed that it is desirable to re-examine the region of the Lajas route, which lies between Lake Nicaragua and its junction with the Rio del Medio route, with a view to ascertaining whether a considerable amount of the surface drainage now falling into the Pacific cannot be diverted into Lake Nicaragua at a reasonable cost. If this should prove to be practicable, it will allow the safe location of a ship-canal through a summit level of only 43 feet above Lake Nicaragua, but with an increase of length of 149 miles in lieu of a deep cut of 133 feet by the Rio del Medio route, now preferred on account of supposed better conditions of permanency. An object never disregarded in our interoceanic canal surveys was to secure the element of permanency, especially from floods, in as great a degree as possible; hence the Rio del Medio route was preferred. The estimate of the cost of this route was 65,722,147 dols., and of the Lajas route 60,352,789, making a difference in the estimates of 5,369,360, with the disadvantage of troublesome surface-water on the Lajas route. It was not supposed, however, that the very careful location of the work when the construction was made might not end in a preference for that route. In my report to the Secretary of the Navy, as chief of the Bureau of Navigation in 1875, will be found the following:—It is proper to add that the most careful and elaborate surveys would necessarily have to be made in advance of any point heretofore examined, before commencing the construction of an interoceanic ship-canal, and that these surveys could only lessen the labour and cost of construction, inasmuch as the locations as given are actual throughout their length, and would only be changed when advantage could be gained by doing so. While a company organized for the purpose of constructing a ship-canal would not fail to relocate every part of the route, a preliminary examination by Civil Engineer Ménocal may show in advance that the surface-drainage above alluded to may advantageously be thrown into Lake Nicaragua, with a considerable decrease in the aggregate estimate for labour, in the substitution of the lower lines of levels of the Lajas routes, and without any sacrifice of the conditions of permanency.'"

We should advise Mr. Ménocal to cause careful series of observations to be made throughout the proposed route with the *Cecchi* seismograph, which has been found so successful in Italy. A detailed account of this remarkable instrument has been given in the January number of the 'Elettricista'

(1877), and a simpler adaptation of this apparatus can be obtained for a small sum, not exceeding twenty dollars.

With regard to the theory of upheaval of the Nicaraguan lakes, it may be noted that, from an investigation of the *fauna* of these waters, made by Dr. Gill and Dr. Bransford, there has been found an interesting association of characteristic marine forms with freshwater types.

Thus, together with *Cichlids* and *Characinæ*, none of which are marine, we have a species of *Megzlops*, a shark, and a saw-fish. The *Megalops* is not known elsewhere in fresh water so isolated from the sea as Lake Nicaragua. The most probable cause of such a combination is the detention and survival of saltwater fishes in inlets of the sea that have become isolated and gradually transformed into freshwater lakes.

MEETING OF THE BRITISH ASSOCIATION, SHEFFIELD.

SECTION G.—MECHANICAL SCIENCE.

This Section resumed its sittings yesterday morning, in the Church Institute, under the chairmanship of Mr. J. Robinson, the President, who was supported by Mr. E. A. Cowper, Mr. Atchison, M.A., Mr. E. Bainbridge, Mr. C. Bergeron, Captain Galton, Mr. Taiso Masaki, Captain Bedford Pim, M.P., R.N., Mr. R. B. Grantham, and others.

There was a large audience assembled for the purpose of hearing a paper from Captain BEDFORD PIM, R.N., M.P., on the proposed canal across the Isthmus of Panama. He said the whole world agreed that the accomplishment of interoceanic canalization of the isthmus of Central America was only a question of time. No one disputes the possibility of making such a canal, and it was generally acknowledged that it might be made a paying concern. The congress on interoceanic canalization did not deal practically with the subject, and the enthusiasm which was so important an element in the greatness of the French people, blinded those who took part in the Congress to the magnitudes and the difficulties of the task, and to the fact that the work already done by M. Lesseps bore about the same relation to the proposed Panama Canal that a small tunnel in the north of France would to that of the Mont Cenis. The physical geography of that part was never taken into consideration; and he was bound to say that the vote in favour of a canal parallel to the Panama Railway was due rather to a personal feeling than to any capability possessed by the route selected. In fact it was rumoured that the process known by our cousins across the Atlantic as "lobbying" was by no means neglected on this occasion; it was not therefore surprising that the American representatives expressed their feelings in terms of the strongest, and, not content with that, made any thing but a favourable report to their own Government. It was not alone the physical difficulty of the undertaking, or even its cost, to which attention should be given. The choice of a route depended upon far more important considerations than those—the terminal ports or harbours for instance. A still more important feature was the physical geography of the sea in the neighbourhood of the ports; for if sailing-ships would be able freely to enter and depart, the success of the undertaking was secured. At least half of England's 21,000 sailing-ships would use the canal; but if Nature placed an irresistible barrier to the approach of these ships, a deep shadow would be cast upon the future outlook of the undertaking. Commodore Maury had said "that if Nature, by one of her convulsions, should rend the continent of America in twain, and make a channel across the Isthmus of Panama or Darien as deep as wide, and as free as the

Straits of Dover, it would never become a commercial thoroughfare for sailing-vessels;" and he indorsed that opinion, for of all parts of the world the calms in the Bay of Panama were the most vexatious and enduring. It therefore became the duty of the Central-American Canal projector to avoid that locality; and, relying upon Commodore Maury, the route from the Atlantic by way of the magnificent Nicaragua lakes to the harbour of Realejo seemed that which was adapted for the required purpose; for it would be quite impossible to exaggerate the money value of having a fair start and approach by means of the little monsoons which blow on that coast. The great difficulty to be overcome in the construction of a canal across Nicaragua was the making and maintaining the harbour of Greytown on its Atlantic terminus, as a strong norther was sufficient to close it, while a high river would reopen an entrance. He thought the cost of the enterprise would paralyze the enterprise, and he would suggest an alternative route parallel to the river San Juan, with a canal of very different dimensions to, and cost of, that at present contemplated. Starting from Monkey Point, now called Pim's Bay, 40 miles north of Greytown, he would cut a canal from the inner part of the bay down to the Rama River, a distance of some 9 miles. The Rama River itself carried deep water some 20 miles into the interior, and the remaining 70 miles, to the lake of Nicaragua, would traverse land offering no particular difficulty. From San Miguelito, on lake Nicaragua, by way of Tipitata to the northern shores of lake Nicaragua, there was nothing which an engineer would consider a difficulty, and the remainder of the canal to Port Realejo could scarcely be said to afford any field for engineering skill. In that scheme a deep-water canal was not even contemplated. A depth of eight feet would be amply sufficient, the vessels being transported on pontoons, such as had been successfully used in the Victoria Docks for some years. Such a plan would considerably reduce the cost, while other advantages would be gained, such as cleaning the ship's bottom while on the pontoon, which would effect a saving to owners almost if not quite sufficient to pay the canal dues. The canal would not cost more than ten millions. If England and America would join hands, and each guarantee 1½ per cent. on that amount, there would be a joint guarantee of 3 per cent., an indication sufficient for English investors alone to take up the sum in less than a week. What was 1½ per cent. on ten millions? £150,000 a year, a sum annually wasted on any vote exceeding one million of the navy estimates. And what did we get for our money? a consolidation of the friendly feeling between this country and the United States far more lasting and binding than could be effected by any treaty between the two nations, merely guaranteeing the neutrality of the route. The representative of the American Government at the Paris Congress left no room for doubt as to the line of canal preferred by his Government, and clearly and unmistakably pointed to Nicaragua as the best. He (Captain Pim) trusted the Government of this country would not, for the sake of saving the annual part of £150,000 for a few years, find themselves ultimately compelled to purchase an interest in the new highway at any price which might then be demanded. He most earnestly hoped that the day would not be far distant when we should see the completion of the great work of interoceanic canalization across Central America. He believed such an undertaking would give a beneficial stimulus to the commerce of the whole world, and, consequently, could not fail to be a great and common boon to mankind. (Applause.)

Mons. Bergeron said that there were a great many objections made to M. de Lesseps's scheme, and very few engineers but were opposed to it. He quite agreed with the deductions of Captain Pim.

Captain GALTON had always thought that one of the great difficulties of M. de Lesseps's canal was the sanitary question—how they would contrive to cut a canal of that size in such a climate. The loss of life would be such that it would be absolutely impossible to carry on the work. In fact, the making of the Panama Railway caused a terrible loss of life. When excavations were made in tropical soils, one always came across an immense amount of decayed vegetation, and the chance of death thereby multiplied. There was one point he should like to ask Captain Pim about, and that was, whether it was necessary, in the Nicaraguan system, to raise ships by means of pontoons in order to carry them across certain distances? That seemed to him to interpose enormous difficulties in the work of the canal. There was, first of all, the objection that many shipowners would raise to having their cargo-laden ships taken out of the water. Then, in the case of so transporting vessels, each ship would have to be accompanied by a subsidiary machine to take it across. The canal, to be universally applicable, must be as simple and effective as possible. Every one must join with Captain Bedford Pim in the hope that something would be done to give us a canal across this space as soon as possible. (Applause.)

Mr. R. B. GRANTHAM pointed out that the mode of transporting ships through the canal as proposed by the author of the paper, though easy enough in the Victoria Docks, would be another matter through the Nicaraguan Canal. Captain Pim had not stated why the proposed canal should not have a greater depth than eight feet. It would be a matter for consideration whether the pontoons would not be so expensive as to overbalance the expense of a greater depth.

Mr. COWPER pointed out that a pontoon large enough to transport a laden ship through the canal would necessarily have a very great displacement, so that the pontoons would have to be large, and so would the canal.

Captain PIM said that he had only suggested the shallow canal because he feared that it would be impossible so to improve the delta of the San Juan River as to make it a proper harbour. Of course every one would prefer to sail through the canal than to have to be hoisted through on a pontoon. A pontoon with a large ship on it would only draw four feet of water. He had seen laden ships easily raised on a pontoon. His suggestion was merely made on the supposition that the delta of the San Juan could not be improved, but he did not of course for a moment presume to say that it was the right one. A deep-water canal through the route he had mentioned would cost £30,000,000 sterling, a sum sufficiently large to frighten both Great Britain and America. A shallow canal, such as the one he had suggested, would cost about £10,000,000 sterling. Of course, if the smaller scheme were carried out, it could afterwards be improved.

A cordial vote of thanks was presented to Captain Pim for his interesting paper.

Philadelphia, Aug. 27.

Admiral Ammen writes that the condition of American feeling respecting the Panama Ship Canal has been communicated to General Grant, and that he has been requested to aid in the construction of a canal *viâ* Nicaragua, and asked whether, if invited by the Directors of a responsible Interoceanic Canal Company having proper concessions, he would serve as President of the Company. Admiral Ammen says he has received a telegram from General Grant consenting to serve. This has been communicated to the Nicaraguan Government, with a request for a concession, which they doubtless will give.

PRINTED BY TAYLOR AND FRANCIS, RED LION COURT, FLEET STREET.